# Weather and Climate Inventory
# National Park Service
# Rocky Mountain Network

Natural Resource Technical Report NPS/ROMN/NRTR—2007/036
WRCC Report 2007-11

Christopher A. Davey, Kelly T. Redmond, and David B. Simeral
Western Regional Climate Center
Desert Research Institute
2215 Raggio Parkway
Reno, Nevada 89512-1095

May 2007

U.S. Department of the Interior
National Park Service
Natural Resource Program Center
Fort Collins, Colorado

The Natural Resource Publication series addresses natural resource topics that are of interest and applicability to a broad readership in the National Park Service and to others in the management of natural resources, including the scientific community, the public, and the National Park Service conservation and environmental constituencies. Manuscripts are peer-reviewed to ensure that the information is scientifically credible, technically accurate, appropriately written for the intended audience, and designed and published in a professional manner.

The Natural Resources Technical Reports series is used to disseminate the peer-reviewed results of scientific studies in the physical, biological, and social sciences for both the advancement of science and the achievement of the National Park Service mission. The reports provide contributors with a forum for displaying comprehensive data that are often deleted from journals because of page limitations. Current examples of such reports include the results of research that address natural resource management issues; natural resource inventory and monitoring activities; resource assessment reports; scientific literature reviews; and peer-reviewed proceedings of technical workshops, conferences, or symposia.

Views and conclusions in this report are those of the authors and do not necessarily reflect policies of the National Park Service. Mention of trade names or commercial products does not constitute endorsement or recommendation for use by the National Park Service.

Printed copies of reports in these series may be produced in a limited quantity and they are only available as long as the supply lasts. This report is also available from the Natural Resource Publications Management website (http://www.nature.nps.gov/publications/NRPM) on the Internet or by sending a request to the address on the back cover.

Please cite this publication as follows:

Davey, C. A., K. T. Redmond, and D. B. Simeral. 2007. Weather and Climate Inventory, National Park Service, Rocky Mountain Network. Natural Resource Technical Report NPS/ROMN/NRTR—2007/036. National Park Service, Fort Collins, Colorado.

NPS/ROMN/NRTR—2007/036, May 2007

# Contents

# Contents (continued)

# Figures

# Tables

# Appendixes

# Acronyms

| | |
|---|---|
| AASC | American Association of State Climatologists |
| ACIS | Applied Climate Information System |
| AgriMet | Pacific Northwest Cooperative Agricultural Network |
| ASOS | Automated Surface Observing System |
| AWOS | Automated Weather Observing System |
| BLM | Bureau of Land Management |
| BWFO | NWS Forecast Office, Boulder, Colorado |
| CANADA | Canadian weather/climate stations |
| CASTNet | Clean Air Status and Trends Network |
| CDOT | Colorado Department of Transportation |
| COOP | Cooperative Observer Program |
| CRBFC | Colorado River Basin Forecast Center |
| CRN | Climate Reference Network |
| CWOP | Citizen Weather Observer Program |
| DFIR | Double-Fence Intercomparison Reference |
| DST | daylight savings time |
| DUDFCD | Denver Urban Drainage and Flood Control District |
| ENSO | El Niño Southern Oscillation |
| EPA | Environmental Protection Agency |
| FAA | Federal Aviation Administration |
| FIPS | Federal Information Processing Standards |
| FLFO | Florissant Fossil Beds National Monument |
| GLAC | Glacier National Park |
| GMT | Greenwich Mean Time |
| GOES | Geostationary Operational Environmental Satellite |
| GNP | Glacier National Park network |
| GPMP | NPS Gaseous Pollutant Monitoring Program |
| GPS | Global Positioning System |
| GPS-MET | NOAA ground-based GPS meteorology |
| GRKO | Grant-Kohrs Ranch National Historic Site |
| GRSA | Great Sand Dunes National Park and Preserve |
| I&M | NPS Inventory and Monitoring Program |
| LEO | Low Earth Orbit |
| LIBI | Little Bighorn Battlefield National Monument |
| LST | local standard time |
| LTER | U.S. Long Term Ecological Research Network |
| MDN | Mercury Deposition Network |
| MSOWFO | NWS Forecast Office, Missoula, Montana |
| MT DOT | Montana Department of Transportation |
| NADP | National Atmospheric Deposition Program |
| NAMS | North America Monsoon System |
| NASA | National Aeronautics and Space Administration |
| NCDC | National Climatic Data Center |
| NetCDF | Network Common Data Form |

| | |
|---|---|
| NOAA | National Oceanic and Atmospheric Administration |
| NPS | National Park Service |
| NRCS | Natural Resources Conservation Service |
| NRCS-SC | NRCS snowcourse network |
| NWS | National Weather Service |
| PDO | Pacific Decadal Oscillation |
| PNA | Pacific-North America Oscillation |
| POMS | Portable Ozone Monitoring System |
| PRISM | Parameter Regression on Independent Slopes Model |
| RAWS | Remote Automated Weather Station network |
| RCC | regional climate center |
| ROMN | Rocky Mountain Inventory and Monitoring Network |
| ROMO | Rocky Mountain National Park |
| SAO | Surface Airways Observation network |
| SCAN | Soil Climate Analysis Network |
| SNOTEL | Snowfall Telemetry network |
| SOD | Summary Of the Day |
| Surfrad | Surface Radiation Budget network |
| USDA | U.S. Department of Agriculture |
| USGS | U.S. Geological Survey |
| UTC | Coordinated Universal Time |
| WBAN | Weather Bureau Army Navy |
| WMO | World Meteorological Organization |
| WRCC | Western Regional Climate Center |
| WX4U | Weather For You network |

# Executive Summary

Climate is a dominant factor driving the physical and ecologic processes affecting the Rocky Mountain Inventory and Monitoring Network (ROMN). The ROMN encompasses a wide range of climates, including dry, continental climates and cold, moist montane and alpine climates. Climatic and physical processes in alpine and subalpine systems influence both the physiology and growth of nearly all organisms in the alpine. Climate is also a primary driver for grassland ecosystems. Extended drought conditions in recent years across much of the ROMN have highlighted the importance of fire as a driver in the grassland and montane systems of the ROMN. Climate changes are likely to have a significant impact in the Rocky Mountains over the next few decades, with effects that include reduced snowpack and glacier extent, increased fire frequency and intensity, and increasing exotic plant invasions and plant pest outbreaks. Because of its influence on the ecology of ROMN park units and the surrounding areas, climate was identified as a high-priority vital sign for ROMN and is one of the 12 basic inventories to be completed for all National Park Service (NPS) Inventory and Monitoring Program (I&M) networks.

This project was initiated to inventory past and present climate monitoring efforts in the ROMN. In this report, we provide the following information:

- Overview of broad-scale climatic factors important to ROMN park units.
- Inventory of weather and climate station locations in and near ROMN park units relevant to the NPS I&M Program.
- Results of an inventory of metadata on each weather station, including affiliations for weather-monitoring networks, types of measurements recorded at these stations, and information about the actual measurements (length of record, etc.).
- Initial evaluation of the adequacy of coverage for existing weather stations and recommendations for improvements in monitoring weather and climate.

Topography is a primary factor defining ROMN climate characteristics, with higher elevations being cooler and wetter. Mean annual precipitation is lowest in western Great Sand Dunes National Park and Preserve (GRSA), at under 200 mm, and is highest in the mountain settings of Glacier National Park (GLAC) and Rocky Mountain National Park (ROMO), where mean annual precipitation can reach over 2000 mm. Because the Rockies are oriented generally perpendicular to the prevailing westerly winds there are extreme east-west climate gradients of precipitation and temperature in the winter months. During the winter months, precipitation in the ROMN is associated with organized storm systems from the west and is deposited mostly on the western slopes. Much of this moisture falls as snow. In summer, precipitation is more convective in nature as the prevailing westerly wind flow weakens and subtropical moisture invades the region from the south. The greatest summer precipitation totals occur in the higher elevations of both GLAC and ROMO. Western slopes can get substantial precipitation all year long, while dryer, lower elevations and east slopes see a summertime precipitation maximum. The mountainous environment over much of the ROMN generally leads to very cool conditions for the year as a whole. The coolest locations, including GLAC and ROMO, have mean annual temperatures that are right around 0°C, while the warmest park units in the ROMN see mean annual temperatures that are not much above 4°C. Most park units in the ROMN have minimum temperatures that generally get below -15°C during the heart of the winter. Maximum summer temperatures at lower elevations often get above 30°C, while cooler mountain areas struggle to get above 15°C.

Through a search of national databases and inquiries to NPS staff, we have identified 58 weather and climate stations within ROMN park units. Glacier National Park (GLAC) has the most stations within park boundaries (33). Most weather and climate stations we identified had metadata and data records that are sufficiently complete and satisfactory in quality.

Various weather/climate networks identified in and around ROMN park units provide climate data suitable for various types of research projects. Local automated networks in and near GLAC and ROMO document the unique climate conditions experienced in alpine environments.

The recent loss of active long-term climate records around some ROMN park units negatively affects the ability to document climate changes across the ROMN. These losses are particularly noticeable in Florissant Fossil Beds National Monument (FLFO), GLAC, and ROMO. Some long-term records identified in this report may actually come from multiple stations. Caution must be exercised when utilizing such records.

Weather/climate station coverage in GLAC is primarily at and near Many Glacier, the main east and west entrances, and around the periphery of the park unit. Station coverage is lacking in northwestern and southern GLAC. The park unit has a local network of near-real-time stations that could be expanded into these unsampled areas. The NPS could also consider working with local agencies to install RAWS (Remote Automated Weather Station) and/or SNOTEL (Snowfall Telemetry network) sites in these areas.

Near-real-time weather data are not available in immediate vicinity of Grant-Kohrs Ranch National Historic Site (GRKO). Due to the largely agricultural setting around GRKO, NPS could consider working with the Natural Resources Conservation Service (NRCS) to install a SCAN (Soil Climate Analysis Network) station in the area.

Both FLFO and Little Bighorn Battlefield National Monument (LIBI) appear to have satisfactory station coverage for their purposes, with the presence of both near-real-time weather stations and long-term climate stations. NPS could consider installing a RAWS station in FLFO and thus expanding the coverage of the RAWS network southward into the FLFO region.

The majority of stations we have identified for ROMO are concentrated at the east and west entrances of the park unit and along Trail Ridge Road (U.S. Highway 34). The extreme northern and southwestern parts of ROMO remain largely unsampled. In these areas, the NPS may want to consider partnering with NRCS to transition existing NRCS-SC sites into SNOTEL sites.

Weather/climate station coverage within GRSA is largely non-existent away from the main visitor center. The NPS may want to consider new RAWS installations in southwestern GRSA station (e.g., near 6N Lane and/or Medano Road) and along the jeep road that runs north and east of the visitor center. Additional SNOTEL stations at the higher elevations of GRSA would also be useful.

# Acknowledgements

This work was supported and completed under Task Agreement H8R07010001, with the Great Basin Cooperative Ecosystem Studies Unit. We would like to acknowledge very helpful assistance from various National Park Service personnel associated with the Rocky Mountain Inventory and Monitoring Network. Particular thanks are extended to Mike Britten and Brent Frakes. We also thank John Gross, Margaret Beer, Grant Kelly, Greg McCurdy, and Heather Angeloff for all their help. Seth Gutman with the National Oceanic and Atmospheric Administration Earth Systems Research Laboratory provided valuable input on the GPS-MET station network. Portions of the work were supported by the NOAA Western Regional Climate Center.

# 1.0. Introduction

Weather and climate are key drivers in ecosystem structure and function. Global- and regional-scale climate variations will have a tremendous impact on natural systems (Chapin et al. 1996; Schlesinger 1997; Jacobson et al. 2000; Bonan 2002). Proper understanding of ecosystem dynamics requires an understanding of the roles of climate variability, hydrologic interactions with soils, and adaptive strategies of biota to capitalize on spatially and temporally variable climate dynamics (Rodriguez-Iturbe 2000). Long-term patterns in temperature and precipitation provide first-order constraints on potential ecosystem structure and function. Secondary constraints are realized from the intensity and duration of individual weather events and, additionally, from seasonality and inter-annual climate variability. These constraints influence the fundamental properties of ecologic systems, such as soil–water relationships, plant–soil processes, and nutrient cycling, as well as disturbance rates and intensity. These properties, in turn, influence the life-history strategies supported by a climatic regime (Neilson 1987; Rodriguez-Iturbe 2000; Britten et al. 2005).

Given the importance of climate, it is one of 12 basic inventories to be completed by the National Park Service (NPS) Inventory and Monitoring Program (I&M) network (I&M 2006). As primary environmental drivers for the other vital signs, weather and climate patterns present various practical and management consequences and implications for the NPS (Oakley et al. 2003). Most park units observe weather and climate elements as part of their overall mission. The lands under NPS stewardship provide many excellent locations for monitoring climatic conditions.

It is essential that park units within the Rocky Mountain Inventory and Monitoring Network (ROMN) have an effective climate-monitoring system in place to track climate changes and to aid in management decisions relating to these changes. The purpose of this report is to determine the current status of weather and climate monitoring within the ROMN (Table 1.1; Figure 1.1). In this report, we provide the following informational elements:

- Overview of broad-scale climatic factors important to ROMN park units.
- Inventory of locations for all weather stations in and near ROMN park units that are relevant to the NPS I&M networks.
- Results of metadata inventory for each station, including weather-monitoring network affiliations, types of recorded measurements, and information about actual measurements (length of record, etc.).
- Initial evaluation of the adequacy of coverage for existing weather stations and recommendations for improvements in monitoring weather and climate.

Table 1.1. Park units in the Rocky Mountain Network.

| Acronym | Name |
|---------|------|
| FLFO | Florissant Fossil Beds National Monument |
| GLAC | Glacier National Park |
| GRKO | Grant-Kohrs Ranch National Historic Site |
| GRSA | Great Sand Dunes National Park and Preserve |
| LIBI | Little Bighorn Battlefield National Monument |
| ROMO | Rocky Mountain National Park |

Figure 1.1. Map of the Rocky Mountain Network.

## 1.1. Network Terminology

Before proceeding, it is important to stress that this report discusses the idea of "networks" in two different ways. Modifiers are used to distinguish between NPS I&M networks and weather/climate station networks. See Appendix A for a full definition of these terms.

### 1.1.1. Weather/Climate Station Networks

Most weather and climate measurements are made not from isolated stations but from stations that are part of a network operated in support of a particular mission. The limiting case is a network of one station, where measurements are made by an interested observer or group. Larger networks usually have additional inventory data and station-tracking procedures. Some national weather/climate networks are associated with the National Oceanic and Atmospheric Administration (NOAA), including the National Weather Service (NWS) Cooperative Observer Program (COOP). Other national networks include the interagency Remote Automated Weather Station network (RAWS) and the U.S. Department of Agriculture/Natural Resources Conservation Service (USDA/NRCS) Snowfall Telemetry (SNOTEL) and snowcourse networks. Usually a single agency, but sometimes a consortium of interested parties, will jointly support a particular weather/climate network.

### 1.1.2. NPS I&M Networks

Within the NPS, the system for monitoring various attributes in the participating park units (about 270–280 in total) is divided into 32 NPS I&M networks. These networks are collections of park units grouped together around a common theme, typically geographical.

## 1.2. Weather versus Climate Definitions

It is also important to distinguish whether the primary use of a given station is for weather purposes or for climate purposes. Weather station networks are intended for near-real-time usage, where the precise circumstances of a set of measurements are typically less important. In these cases, changes in exposure or other attributes over time are not as critical. Climate networks, however, are intended for long-term tracking of atmospheric conditions. Siting and exposure are critical factors for climate networks, and it is vitally important that the observational circumstances remain essentially unchanged over the duration of the station record. Some climate networks can be considered hybrids of weather/climate networks. These hybrid climate networks can supply information on a short-term "weather" time scale and a longer-term "climate" time scale.

In this report, "weather" generally refers to current (or near-real-time) atmospheric conditions, while "climate" is defined as the complete ensemble of statistical descriptors for temporal and spatial properties of atmospheric behavior (see Appendix A). Climate also considers how the atmosphere affects and is affected by other systems such as the hydrosphere, cryosphere, biosphere, and lithosphere. Climate and weather phenomena often overlap significantly, with these phenomena shading gradually into each other and ultimately becoming inseparable.

## 1.3. Purpose of Measurements

Climate inventory and monitoring climate activities should be based on a set of guiding fundamental principles. Any evaluation of weather/climate monitoring programs begins with asking the following question:

3

- What is the purpose of weather and climate measurements?

Evaluation of past, present, or planned weather/climate monitoring activities must be based on the answer to this question.

Weather and climate data and information constitute a prominent and widely requested component of the NPS I&M networks (I&M 2006). Within the context of the NPS, the following services constitute the main purposes for recording weather and climate observations:

- Provide measurements for real-time operational needs and early warnings of potential hazards (landslides, mudflows, washouts, fallen trees, plowing activities, fire conditions, aircraft and watercraft conditions, road conditions, rescue conditions, fog, restoration and remediation activities, etc.).
- Provide visitor education and aid interpretation of expected and actual conditions for visitors while they are in the park and for deciding if and when to visit the park.
- Establish engineering and design criteria for structures, roads, culverts, etc., for human comfort, safety, and economic needs.
- Consistently monitor climate over the long-term to detect changes in environmental drivers affecting ecosystems, including both gradual and sudden events.
- Provide retrospective data to understand *a posteriori* changes in flora and fauna.
- Aid in the interpretation of other vital signs/protocols by removing the climate signal.
- Document for posterity the physical conditions in and near the park units, including mean, extreme, and variable measurements (in time and space) for all applications.

The last four items in the preceding list are pertinent primarily to the NPS I&M networks; however, all items are important to NPS operations and management. Most of the needs in this list overlap heavily. It is often impractical to operate separate climate measuring systems that also cannot be used to meet ordinary weather needs, where there is greater emphasis on timeliness and reliability.

### 1.3.1. Who Makes the Measurements?
The lands under NPS stewardship provide many excellent locations to host the monitoring of climate by the NPS or other collaborators. These lands are largely protected from human development and other land changes that can impact observed climate records. Most park units historically have observed weather/climate elements as part of their overall mission. Many of these measurements come from station networks managed by other agencies, with observations taken or overseen by NPS personnel, in some cases, or by collaborators from the other agencies. National Park Service units that are small, lack sufficient resources, or lack sites presenting adequate exposure may benefit by utilizing weather/climate measurements collected from nearby stations.

### 1.4. Design of Climate-Monitoring Programs
Determining the purposes for collecting measurements in a given weather/climate monitoring program will guide the process of identifying weather/climate stations suitable for the monitoring program. The context for making these decisions is provided in Chapter 2 where background on

the ROMN climate is presented. However, this process is only one step in evaluating and designing a climate-monitoring program. The following steps must also be included:

- Define park and network-specific monitoring needs and objectives.
- Determine the spatial and temoral scales at which the surface environment responds to atmospheric processes and variations.
- Identify locations and data repositories of existing and historic stations.
- Acquire existing data when necessary or practical.
- Evaluate the quality of existing data.
- Evaluate the adequacy of coverage of existing stations.
- Develop a protocol for monitoring the weather and climate, including the following:
  o Standardized summaries and reports of weather/climate data.
  o Data management (quality assurance and quality control, archiving, data access, etc.).
- Develop and implement a plan for installing or modifying stations, as necessary.

Throughout the design process, there are various factors that require consideration in evaluating weather and climate measurements. Many of these factors have been summarized by Dr. Tom Karl, director of the NOAA National Climatic Data Center (NCDC), and widely distributed as the "Ten Principles for Climate Monitoring" (Karl et al. 1996; NRC 2001). These principles are presented in Appendix B, and the guidelines are embodied in many of the comments made throughout this report.

The aforementioned design considerations for weather/ climate-monitoring programs are discussed further in the following subsections. In addition, an overview of requirements necessary to operate a climate network is provided in Appendix C, with further discussion in Appendix D.

### 1.4.1. Need for Consistency
A principal goal in climate monitoring is to detect and characterize slow and sudden changes in climate through time. This is of less concern for day-to-day weather changes, but it is of paramount importance for climate variability and change. There are many ways whereby changes in techniques for making measurements, changes in instruments or their exposures, or seemingly innocuous changes in site characteristics can lead to apparent changes in climate. Safeguards must be in place to avoid these false sources of temporal "climate" variability if we are to draw correct inferences about climate behavior over time from archived measurements.

For climate monitoring, consistency through time is vital, counting at least as important as absolute accuracy. Sensors record only what is occurring at the sensor—this is all they can detect. It is the responsibility of station or station network managers to ensure that observations are representative of the spatial and temporal climate scales that we wish to record.

### 1.4.2. Metadata
Changes in instruments, site characteristics, and observing methodologies can lead to apparent changes in climate through time. It is therefore vital to document all factors that can bear on the interpretation of climate measurements and to update the information repeatedly through time. This information ("metadata," data about data) has its own history and set of quality-control

5

issues that parallel those of the actual data. There is no single standard for the content of climate metadata, but a simple rule suffices:

- Observers should record all information that could be needed in the future to interpret observations correctly without benefit of the observers' personal recollections.

Such documentation includes notes, drawings, site forms, and photos, which can be of inestimable value if taken in the correct manner. That stated, it is not always clear to the metadata provider *what is important* for posterity and *what will be important* in the future. It is almost impossible to "over document" a station. Station documentation is greatly underappreciated and is seldom thorough enough (especially for climate purposes). Insufficient attention to this issue often lowers the present and especially future value of otherwise useful data.

The convention followed throughout climatology is to refer to metadata as information about the measurement process, station circumstances, and data. The term "data" is reserved solely for the actual weather and climate records obtained from sensors.

### 1.4.3. Maintenance

Inattention to maintenance is the greatest source of failure in weather/climate stations and networks. Problems begin to occur soon after sites are deployed. A regular visit schedule must be implemented, where sites, settings (e.g., vegetation), sensors, communications, and data flow are checked routinely (once or twice a year at a minimum) and updated as necessary. Parts must be changed out for periodic recalibration or replacement. With adequate maintenance, the entire instrument suite should be replaced or completely refurbished about once every five to seven years.

Simple preventive maintenance is effective but requires much planning and skilled technical staff. Changes in technology and products require retraining and continual re-education. Travel, logistics, scheduling, and seasonal access restrictions consume major amounts of time and budget but are absolutely necessary. Without such attention, data gradually become less credible and then often are misused or not used at all.

### 1.4.4. Automated versus Manual Stations

Historic stations often have depended on manual observations and many continue to operate in this mode. Manual observations frequently produce excellent data sets. Sensors and data are simple and intuitive, well tested, and relatively cheap. Manual stations have much to offer in certain circumstances and can be a source of both primary and backup data. However, methodical consistency for manual measurements is a constant challenge, especially with a mobile work force. Operating manual stations takes time and needs to be done on a regular schedule, though sometimes the routine is welcome.

Nearly all newer stations are automated. Automated stations provide better time resolution, increased (though imperfect) reliability, greater capacity for data storage, and improved accessibility to large amounts of data. The purchase cost for automated stations is higher than for manual stations. A common expectation and serious misconception is that an automated station

6

can be deployed and left to operate on its own. In reality, automation does not eliminate the need for people but rather changes the type of person that is needed. Skilled technical personnel are needed and must be readily available, especially if live communications exist and data gaps are not wanted. Site visits are needed at least annually and spare parts must be maintained. Typical annual costs for sensors and maintenance are $1500–2500 per station per year but these costs still can vary greatly depending on the kind of automated site.

### 1.4.5. Communications

With manual stations, the observer is responsible for recording and transmitting station data. Data from automated stations, however, can be transmitted quickly for access by research and operations personnel, which is a highly preferable situation. A comparison of communication systems for automated and manual stations shows that automated stations generally require additional equipment, more power, higher transmission costs, attention to sources of disruption or garbling, and backup procedures (e.g., manual downloads from data loggers).

Automated stations are capable of functioning normally without communication and retaining many months of data. At such sites, however, alerts about station problems are not possible, large gaps can accrue when accessible stations quit, and the constituencies needed to support such stations are smaller and less vocal. Two-way communications permit full recovery from disruptions, ability to reprogram data loggers remotely, and better opportunities for diagnostics and troubleshooting. In virtually all cases, two-way communications are much preferred to all other communication methods. However, two-way communications require considerations of cost, signal access, transmission rates, interference, and methods for keeping sensor and communication power loops separate. Two-way communications are frequently impossible (no service) or impractical, expensive, or power consumptive. Two-way methods (cellular, land line, radio, Internet) require smaller up-front costs as compared to other methods of communication and have variable recurrent costs, starting at zero. Satellite links work everywhere (except when blocked by trees or cliffs) and are quite reliable but are one-way and relatively slow, allow no re-transmissions, and require high up-front costs ($3000–4000) but no recurrent costs. Communications technology is changing constantly and requires vigilant attention by maintenance personnel.

### 1.4.6. Quality Assurance and Quality Control

Quality control and quality assurance are issues at every step through the entire sequence of sensing, communication, storage, retrieval, and display of environmental data. Quality assurance is an umbrella concept that covers all data collection and processing (start-to-finish) and ensures that credible information is available to the end user. Quality control has a more limited scope and is defined by the International Standards Organization as "the operational techniques and activities that are used to satisfy quality requirements." The central problem can be better appreciated if we approach quality control in the following way.

- Quality control is the evaluation, assessment, and rehabilitation of imperfect data by utilizing other imperfect data.

The quality of the data only decreases with time once the observation is made. The best and most effective quality control, therefore, consists in making high-quality measurements from the start, ingesting this data either by live or periodic data collection, and then successfully transmitting the data to a storage site. Once the data are received from a monitoring station, a series of checks with increasing complexity can be applied, ranging from single-element checks (self-consistency) to multiple-element checks (inter-sensor consistency) to multiple-station/single-element checks (inter-station consistency). Suitable ancillary data (battery voltages, data ranges for all measurements, etc.) can prove extremely useful in diagnosing problems.

There is rarely a single technique in quality control procedures that will work satisfactorily for all situations. Quality-control procedures must be tailored to individual station circumstances, data access and storage methods, and climate regimes.

The fundamental issue in quality control centers on the tradeoff between falsely rejecting good data (Type I error) and falsely accepting bad data (Type II error). A reduction in the incidence of one type of error increases the incidence of the other type, and vice versa. In weather and climate data assessments, since good data are absolutely crucial for interpreting climate records properly, Type I errors are deemed far less desirable than Type II errors.

Not all observations are equal in importance. Quality-control procedures are likely to have the greatest difficulty evaluating the most extreme observations, where independent information usually must be sought and incorporated. Quality-control procedures involving more than one station usually involve a great deal of infrastructure with its own (imperfect) error-detection methods, which must be in place before a single value can be evaluated.

### 1.4.7. Standards
Although there is near-universal recognition of the value in systematic weather and climate measurements, these measurements will have little value unless they conform to accepted standards. There is not a single source for standards for collecting weather and climate data nor a single standard that meets all needs. Measurement standards have been developed by the World Meteorological Organization (WMO 1983; 2005), the American Association of State Climatologists (AASC 1985), the U.S. Environmental Protection Agency (EPA 1987), Finklin and Fischer (1990), the RAWS program (Bureau of Land Management [BLM] 1997), and the National Wildfire Coordinating Group (2004). Variations to these measurement standards also have been offered by instrument makers (e.g., Tanner 1990).

# 2.0. Climate Background

The Rocky Mountain Network has determined that climate is a key driver of almost all vital signs likely to be monitored at all ROMN park units (Britten et al. 2005). An understanding of both current climate patterns and climate history in the ROMN is important to understanding and interpreting change and patterns in ecosystem attributes. It is essential that the ROMN park units have an effective climate monitoring system to track climate changes and to aid in management decisions relating to these changes. In order to do this, it is essential to understand the climate characteristics of the ROMN, as discussed in this chapter.

## 2.1. Climate and the ROMN Environment

The ROMN encompasses a wide range of climate settings. In eastern ROMN (e.g., LIBI), cold, dry continental settings are the rule. However, northwestern ROMN is relatively cool and is influenced by moist maritime air masses. Warmer dry temperate settings occur in southernmost ROMN park units (e.g., lower elevations of GRSA).

Climatic and physical processes are perhaps the most important set of drivers in alpine and subalpine systems. While other factors can have significant effects, especially locally, climate is the key limit on the physiology and growth of nearly all organisms in alpine areas (Tranquillini 1979). Temperature and precipitation extremes, coupled with high radiation levels and other factors such as wind (Hadley and Smith 1986), create very severe conditions that commonly disturb alpine substrates and limit plant growth. Wind also drives ice and snow which scour and abrade surfaces and plant tissues, and causes snow to accumulate.

Snow drifts often do not melt away until well into the alpine growing season, limiting early growth stages of alpine plants. Snowpack depth, duration and distribution are important via their influence on moisture content, growing season length, physical damage to vegetation and indirect impacts on nitrogen deposition dynamics. Further, snowpack is critically linked to glacial formation and deterioration, and melt-off from glaciers has important determinant effects on stream, lake, and wetland hydrology and water chemistry.

As with alpine ecosystems, climate has been described as the primary driving variable of grassland ecosystem processes (Frank and McNaughton 1992); however, climatic variation interact with essentially every other driver in grasslands, making its effect complex and often indirect. Climate conditions in grasslands are marked by large variability in temperature and precipitation throughout the year (Borchert 1950). Grasslands are semi-arid, with frequent drought events. These periodic drought events permit vegetation to dry, interacting with the fire regime. Vegetative biomass production is underpinned by temperature and soil moisture availability that are generally controlled temporally by the onset of the growing season (with a cascade of impacts if this is modified via global climate change).

Extended drought conditions in recent years across much of the ROMN have highlighted the importance of fire as a driver in the grassland and montane systems of the ROMN (Britten et al. 2005). In lower elevation sub-alpine forests, lodgepole pine-dominated stands often may be dry enough, on average, to support regular understory fires in addition to periodic stand-replacing events (Gabriel 1976; Fischer and Bradley 1987; Smith and Fischer 1997). This is especially true with those stands infected with mountain pine beetle outbreaks, which have been increasing in extent due to recent mild winters across the ROMN region. Although most alpine and upper subalpine habitats are less common, periodic drought coupled with dense stands (which develop during fire-free periods) can lead to rare, but severe, stand-replacing fires that may burn into alpine systems (Pfister et al. 1977; Arno 1980; Agee 1997).

Climate plays a large role in many aspects of ROMN lotic systems. Changes in climate, both short and long term, can directly and indirectly affect hydrology, temperature, channel morphology and many other aspects of lotic systems. Watershed scale processes and structure typically interacts with climatic variability in many of these relationships (Ziemer and Lisle 1998).

Climate changes are likely to have a significant impact in the Rocky Mountains over the next few decades (NAST 2001; Wagner 2003). Predicting effects of climate change for the ROMN park units are difficult to specify but may include drier, warmer conditions with reduced snowpack (Wagner 2003; Mote et al. 2005). Glaciers have already decreased dramatically over GLAC during the past few decades (Britten et al. 2005), hinting at climate change effects that are already taking place. Possible ecosystem effects include increased fire frequency and intensity (Heyerdahl et al. 2002; Hessl et al. 2004), increased rates of plant invasions, and increased rates and extents of plant pest outbreaks (D'Antonio 2000; Logan and Powell 2001; Whitlock et al. 2003; McKenzie et al. 2004).

## 2.2. Parameter Regression on Independent Slopes Model

The climate maps presented in this report were generated using the Parameter Regression on Independent Slopes Model (PRISM). This model was developed to address the extreme spatial and elevation gradients exhibited by the climate of the western U.S. (Daly et al. 1994; 2002; Gibson et al. 2002; Doggett et al. 2004). The maps produced through PRISM have undergone rigorous evaluation in the western U.S. This model was originally developed to provide climate information at scales matching available land-cover maps to assist in ecologic modeling. The PRISM technique accounts for the scale-dependent effects of topography on mean values of climate elements. Elevation provides the first-order constraint for the mapped climate fields, with slope and orientation (aspect) providing second-order constraints. The model has been enhanced gradually to address inversions, coast/land gradients, and climate patterns in small-scale trapping basins. Monthly climate fields are generated by PRISM to account for seasonal variations in elevation gradients in climate elements. These monthly climate fields then can be combined into seasonal and annual climate fields. Since PRISM maps are grid maps, they do not replicate point values but rather, for a given grid cell, represent the grid-cell average of the climate variable in question at the average elevation for that cell. The model relies on observed surface and upper-air measurements to estimate spatial climate fields.

## 2.3. Spatial Variability

Topography is a primary factor defining ROMN climate characteristics. Integrated annually, lower elevations are drier and warmer than higher elevations, which are cool and wet. This pattern shows up clearly in mean annual precipitation totals for the ROMN parks units (Figure 2.1). The greatest precipitation totals are generally found in the mountain settings of GLAC, where mean annual precipitation can reach over 2000 mm in the highest elevations. Even in the higher elevations of ROMO, annual precipitation totals greater than 1000 mm are not uncommon. In contrast, lower-elevation park units located in the mountain valleys and basins are much drier. The driest conditions in the ROMN are found in western portions of GRSA, where less than 200 mm of precipitation falls each year on average. Even GRKO, located in the upper Clark Fork valley of west-central Montana, receives less than 300 mm each year. The ROMN park units along the eastern edge of the Rocky Mountains (e.g., FLFO and LIBI) generally receive 300-500 mm of precipitation annually.

Because the Rockies are oriented generally perpendicular to the prevailing westerly winds there are extreme east-west climate gradients. This is true with precipitation in particular, where west slopes of the component ranges of the Rockies are generally wetter than east slopes due to orographic uplift and rain shadow effects. In the winter months, storms approaching ROMN park units from the Pacific Ocean are laden with moisture, depositing higher precipitation on the slopes west of the Continental Divide. Much of this moisture falls as snow. Higher elevations of GLAC and ROMN can see over 1500 cm of snow (Figure 2.2). Conversely, the east side of the Rockies often lies in a rainshadow. However, both polar continental cold air from boreal regions and warmer maritime moist air from the Gulf of Mexico occasionally interact with each other during the winter months in association with winter storms. These air masses collide with the Rocky Mountain front and generate precipitation along the eastern slopes of the Rockies (Maddux 1978; Abbs and Pielke 1987; Petersen et al. 1999). These occasional upslope storms impact the network and provide much of the winter precipitation that occurs on the mountain slopes east of the Continental Divide. The number of these upslope events varies greatly interannually, making it difficult to obtain a general estimate of the percentage of winter precipitation that comes from these storms.

During the summer months, however, the prevailing westerly wind flow weakens and subtropical moisture invades the region from the south. The northern Rockies continue to receive occasional weak Pacific systems, with frontal precipitation that is generally light and occurs uniformly over scales of hundreds of kilometers. In contrast, precipitation is more convective towards the south, with much higher spatial variability. Precipitation can occur on scales of a few kilometers or less. These more-localized precipitation events can bring potentially copious amounts of rainfall. Much of this summer convective precipitation is driven in large part by the North American Monsoon System (NAMS; Adams and Comrie 1997; Ropelewski et al. 2005). The greatest summer precipitation totals occur in the higher elevations of both GLAC and ROMO (e.g., see Figure 2.3).

Monthly precipitation distributions can vary dramatically across the mountainous topography of the larger ROMN park units, like GLAC and ROMO. Slopes west of the Continental Divide can get substantially more precipitation in the winter months, compared to slopes east of the Continental Divide. Looking at differences in monthly precipitation patterns between the east and west sides of these larger park units (Figure 2.4), GLAC shows little difference between the east and west sides of the park unit. However, ROMO shows a dramatic east-west difference in monthly precipitation distributions. This is particularly true with respect to winter precipitation. Grand Lake, in western ROMO, receives precipitation fairly evenly through the course of the year, while Estes Park, just east of ROMO, receives very little winter precipitation. The eastern side of ROMO gets the majority of its precipitation in the spring and summer months. The

Figure 2.1. Mean annual precipitation, 1961-1990, for the ROMN.

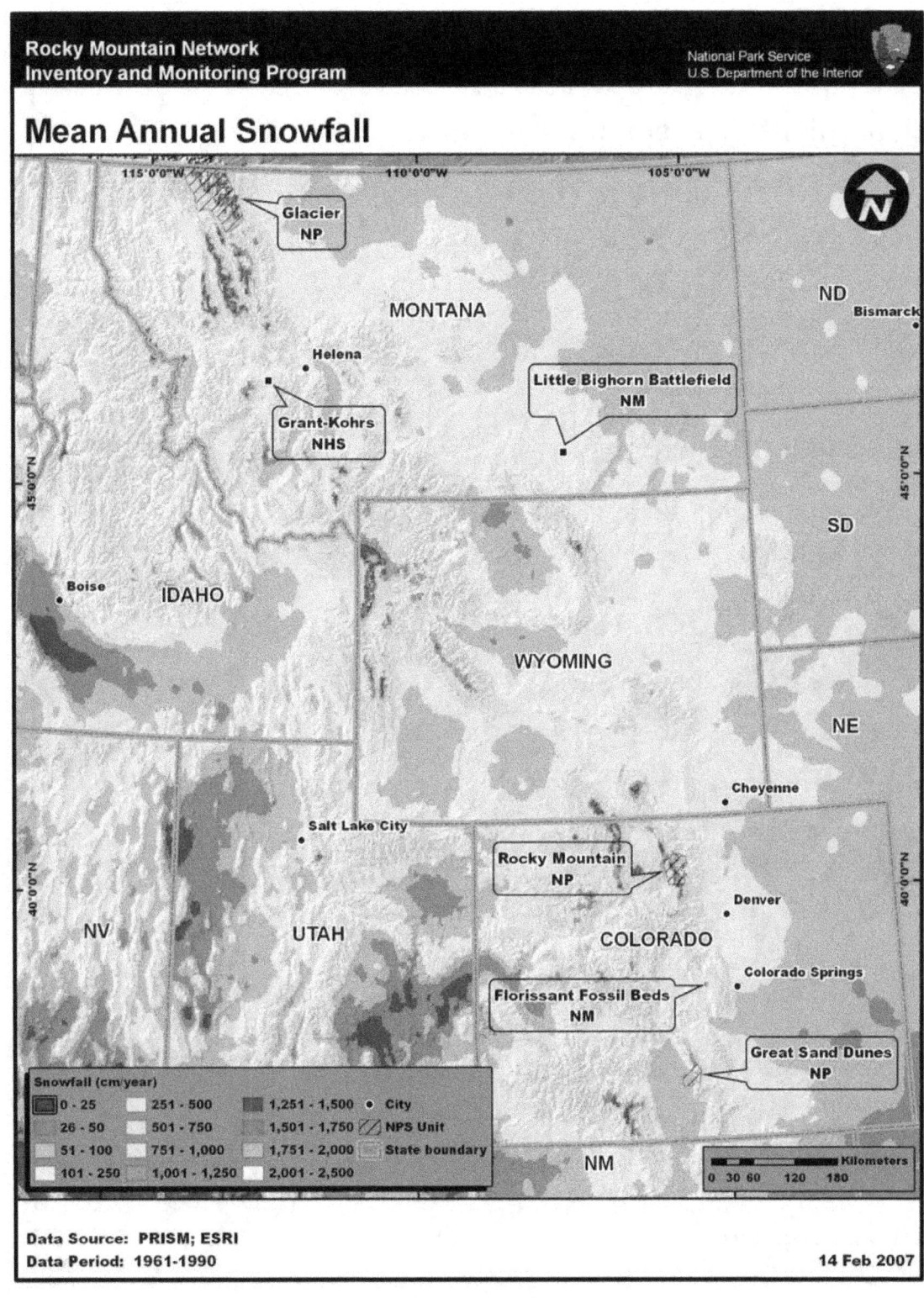

Figure 2.2. Mean annual snowfall, 1961-1990, for the ROMN.

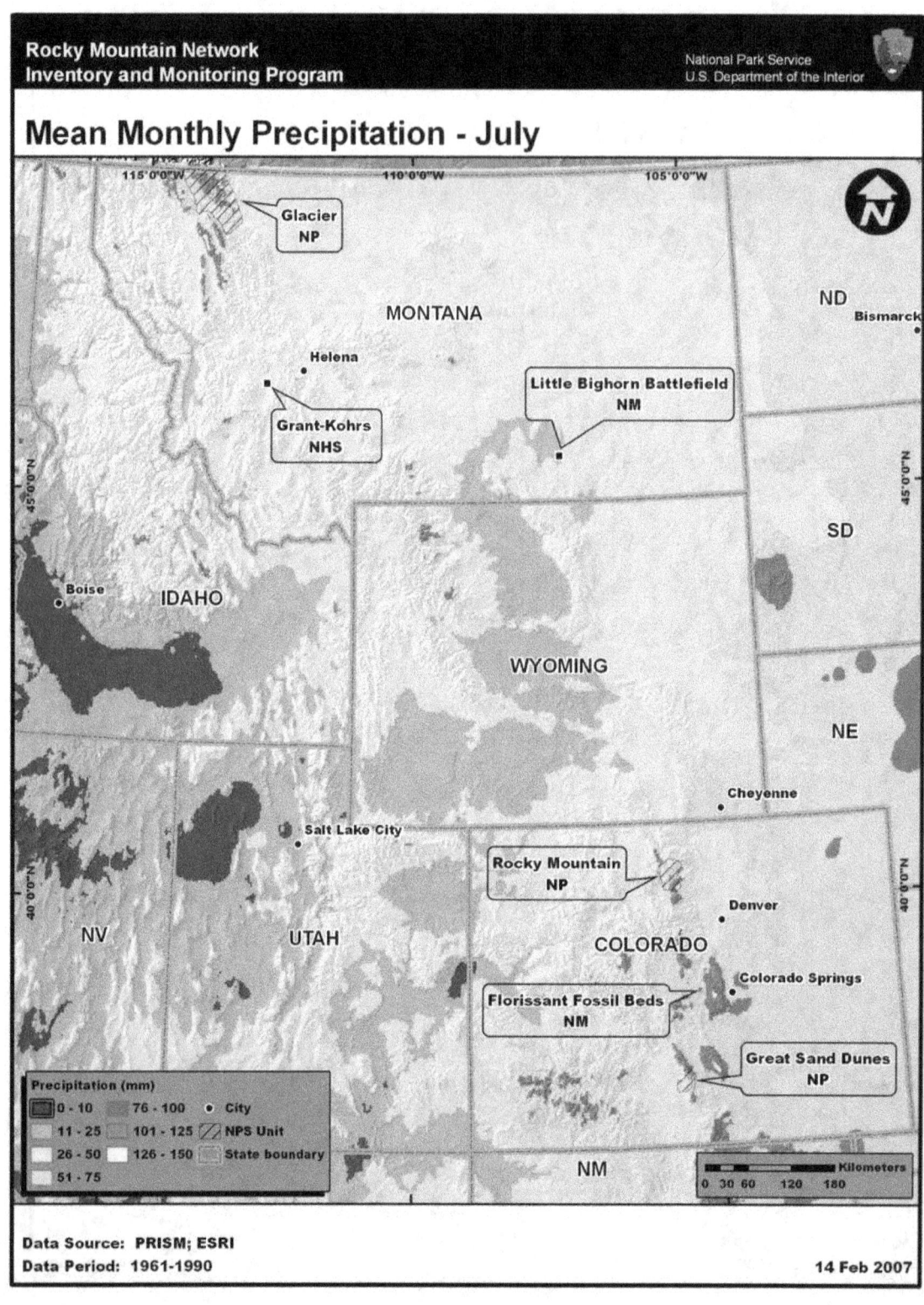

Figure 2.3. Mean July precipitation, 1961-1990, for the ROMN.

Figure 2.4. Mean monthly precipitation at GLAC and ROMO, highlighting east-west variations in precipitation maxima. Panels (a) and (c) are locations on the west sides of GLAC and ROMO, respectively, while panels (b) and (d) are locations on the east sides of GLAC and ROMO, respectively.

15

spring/summer precipitation maximum is also common for lower-elevation ROMN park units, along with those park units that are on the east flanks of the Rocky Mountains. To the north, a warm season precipitation maximum tends to occur in the late spring and early summer (Figure 2.5). As one heads south, however, the influence of NAMS becomes more evident and precipitation maxima occur later in the summer.

a)

b)

Figure 2.5. Monthly precipitation near ROMN park units with summer precipitation maxima. Locations include GRKO (a) and GRSA (b).

16

The mountainous environment over much of the ROMN generally leads to very cool conditions throughout any given year. The coolest locations, including GLAC and ROMO, have mean annual temperatures that are right around 0°C (Figure 2.6). The warmest park units in the ROMN, such as LIBI and much of GRSA, see mean annual temperatures that are not much above 4°C.

Most park units in the ROMN have minimum temperatures that generally get below -15°C during the heart of the winter (Figure 2.7). However, the warmest areas see minimum temperatures that are closer to -10°C. Along the eastern edges of ROMO and, to a lesser extent, the eastern side of GLAC, these warmer conditions are due to downslope winds (with air warming as it descends) from the prevailing westerlies during the winter months. Milder minimums are also found in western GLAC, associated with milder Pacific air accompanying winter storms approaching from the west.

Topography is the primary factor determining summer daytime temperatures throughout the ROMN. In July, for instance, the warmest daytime temperatures are found at LIBI, which is a lower-elevation park unit in southeastern Montana. Maximum temperatures at this location generally get above 30°C (Figure 2.8). In contrast to this, the more mountainous park units like GLAC and ROMO see much cooler daytime temperatures. The coolest summer conditions are found at ROMO, where daytime maximum temperatures generally do not get above 18°C and the highest elevations in the park unit do not get above 15°C.

## 2.4. Temporal Variability

The Pacific-North America Oscillation, or PNA (see Wallace and Gutzler 1981; Barnston and Livezey 1987) is an important contributor to variability of storm frequencies and tracks during a given year across the ROMN. The PNA is characterized by a pressure center in the western Gulf of Alaska and a corresponding pressure center of opposite sign near the U.S. west coast. The PNA varies on the order of weeks. Negative phases of the PNA, characterized by high pressure in the Gulf of Alaska and low pressure along the U.S. west coast, generally bring stormier conditions to the ROMN, particularly to those park units in western Montana.

Both the El Niño-Southern Oscillation (ENSO) and the Pacific Decadal Oscillation (PDO) are ocean-atmosphere feedback mechanisms that cause interannual climate variations in the ROMN (Redmond and Koch 1991; Mock 1996; Cayan et al. 1998; Mantua 2000; Mantua and Hare 2002). El Niño conditions and/or positive phases of the PDO are associated with warmer and drier than normal conditions in northern ROMN, with cooler, wetter conditions in southern ROMN.

Precipitation around the ROMN region over the last century (Figure 2.9) reveals several notable dry and wet periods. For instance, dry periods around 1900 and during the 1930s are evident in much of the ROMN. Colorado precipitation time series (e.g., Figure 2.9c) show a marked dry period during the 1950s as well. The recent dry spell of the late 1990s and early 2000s is evident throughout the ROMN. Temperatures across the ROMN region show a marked warming during the last century (Figure 2.10), with most of this warming occurring in the past few decades. This warming becomes more evident as one moves southward across the ROMN. Warmer conditions are evident during the dry periods of the early 1900s, the 1930s, and the 1950s.

17

Figure 2.6. Mean annual temperature, 1961-1990, for the ROMN.

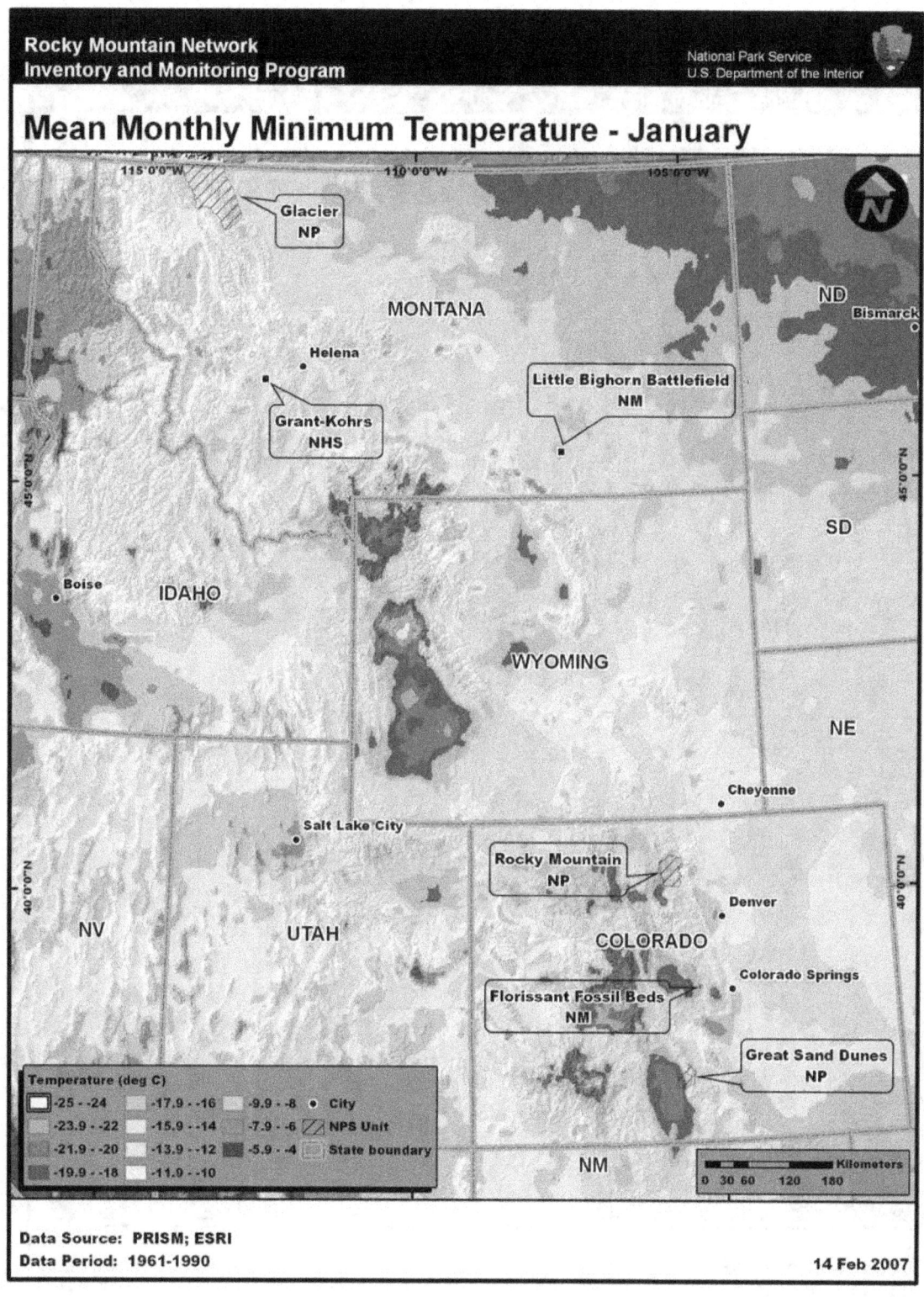

Figure 2.7. Mean January minimum temperature, 1961-1990, for the ROMN.

Figure 2.8. Mean July maximum temperature, 1961-1990, for the ROMN.

a)

b)

c)

Figure 2.9. Precipitation time series, 1895-2005, for selected regions in the ROMN. These include twelve-month precipitation (ending in December) (red), 10-year running mean (blue), mean (green), and plus/minus one standard deviation (green dotted). Locations include western Montana (a), western Colorado (b), and the San Luis valley in Colorado (c).

21

a)

b)

c)

Figure 2.10. Temperature time series, 1895-2005, for selected regions in the ROMN. These include twelve-month average temperature (ending in December) (red), 10-year running mean (blue), mean (green), and plus/minus one standard deviation (green dotted). Locations include western Montana (a), western Colorado (b), and the San Luis valley in Colorado (c).

22

# 3.0. Methods

Having discussed the climatic characteristics of the ROMN and how these can affect the interpretation of station-level data, we now present the procedures that were used to obtain information for weather/climate stations within the ROMN. This information was obtained from various sources, as mentioned in the following paragraphs. Retrieval of station metadata constituted a major component of this work.

## 3.1. Metadata Retrieval

A key component of station inventories is determining the kinds of observations that have been conducted over time, by whom, and in what manner; when each type of observation began and ended; and whether these observations are still being conducted. Metadata about the observational process (Table 3.1) generally consist of a series of vignettes that apply to time intervals and, therefore, constitute a *history* rather than a single snapshot. An expanded list of relevant metadata fields for this inventory is provided in Appendix E. This report has relied on metadata records from three sources: (a) Western Regional Climate Center (WRCC), (b) NPS personnel, and (c) other knowledgeable personnel, such as state climate office staff.

The initial metadata sources for this report were stored at WRCC. This regional climate center (RCC) acts as a working repository of many western climate records, including the main networks outlined in this section. The WRCC conducts live and periodic data collection (ingests) from all major national and western weather/climate networks. These networks include the COOP network, the Surface Airways Observation network (SAO) operated by NWS and the Federal Aviation Administration (FAA), the interagency RAWS network, and various smaller networks. The WRCC is expanding its capability to ingest information from other networks as resources permit and usefulness dictates. This center has relied heavily on historic archives (in many cases supplemented with live ingests) to assess the quantity (not necessarily quality) of data available for NPS I&M network applications.

The primary source of metadata at WRCC is the Applied Climate Information System (ACIS), a joint effort among RCCs and other NOAA entities. Metadata for ROMN weather/climate stations identified from the ACIS database are available in file "ROMN_from_ACIS.tar.gz" (see Appendix F). Historic metadata pertaining to major climate- and weather-observing systems in the U.S. are stored in ACIS where metadata are linked to the observed data. A distributed system, ACIS is synchronized among the RCCs. Mainstream software is utilized, including Postgress, Python™, and Java™ programming languages; CORBA®-compliant network software; and industry-standard, nonproprietary hardware and software. Metadata and data for all major national climate and weather networks have been entered into the ACIS database. For this project, the available metadata from many smaller networks also have been entered but in most cases the actual data have not yet been entered. Data sets are in the NetCDF (Network Common Data Form) format, but the design allows for integration with legacy systems, including non-NetCDF files (used at WRCC) and additional metadata (added for this project). The ACIS also supports a suite of products to visualize or summarize data from these data sets. National climate-monitoring maps are updated daily using the ACIS data feed. The developmental phases of ACIS have utilized metadata supplied by the NCDC and NWS with many tens of thousands of entries, screened as well as possible for duplications, mistakes, and omissions.

Table 3.1. Primary metadata fields for ROMN weather and climate stations. Explanations are provided as appropriate.

| Metadata Field | Notes |
|---|---|
| Station name | Station name associated with network listed in "Climate Network." |
| Latitude | Numerical value (units: see coordinate units). |
| Longitude | Numerical value (units: see coordinate units). |
| Coordinate units | Latitude/longitude (units: decimal degrees, degree-minute-second, etc.). |
| Datum | Datum used as basis for coordinates: WGS 84, NAD 83, etc. |
| Elevation | Elevation of station above mean sea level (m). |
| Slope | Slope of ground surface below station (degrees). |
| Aspect | Azimuth that ground surface below station faces. |
| Climate division | NOAA climate division where station is located. Climate divisions are NOAA-specified zones sharing similar climate and hydrology characteristics. |
| Country | Country where station is located. |
| State | State where station is located. |
| County | County where station is located. |
| Weather/climate network | Primary weather/climate network the station belongs to (COOP, RAWS, etc.). |
| NPS unit code | Four-letter code identifying park unit where station resides. |
| NPS unit name | Full name of park unit. |
| NPS unit type | National park, national monument, etc. |
| UTM zone | If UTM is the only coordinate system available. |
| Location notes | Useful information not already included in "station narrative." |
| Climate variables | Temperature, precipitation, etc. |
| Installation date | Date of station installation. |
| Removal date | Date of station removal. |
| Station photograph | Digital image of station. |
| Photograph date | Date photograph was taken. |
| Photographer | Name of person who took the photograph. |
| Station narrative | Anything related to general site description; may include site exposure, characteristics of surrounding vegetation, driving directions, etc. |
| Contact name | Name of the person involved with station operation. |
| Organization | Group or agency affiliation of contact person. |
| Contact type | Designation that identifies contact person as the station owner, observer, maintenance person, data manager, etc. |
| Position/job title | Official position/job title of contact person. |
| Address | Address of contact person. |
| E-mail address | E-mail address of contact person. |
| Phone | Phone number of contact person (and extension if available). |
| Contact notes | Other information needed to reach contact person. |

Two types of information have been used to complete the ROMN climate station inventory.

- <u>Station inventories</u>: Information about observational procedures, latitude/longitude, elevation, measured elements, measurement frequency, sensor types, exposures, ground cover and vegetation, data-processing details, network, purpose, and managing individual or agency, etc.

- Data inventories: Information about measured data values including completeness, seasonality, data gaps, representation of missing data, flagging systems, how special circumstances in the data record are denoted, etc.

This is not a straightforward process. Extensive searches are typically required to develop historic station and data inventories. Both types of inventories frequently contain information gaps and often rely on tacit and unrealistic assumptions. Sources of information for these inventories frequently are difficult to recover or are undocumented and unreliable. In many cases, the actual weather/climate data available from different sources are not linked directly to metadata records. To the extent that actual data can be acquired (rather than just metadata), it is possible to cross-check these records and perform additional assessments based on the amount and completeness of the data.

Certain types of weather/climate networks that possess any of the following attributes have not been considered for inclusion in the inventory:

- Private networks with proprietary access and/or inability to obtain or provide sufficient metadata.
- Private weather enthusiasts (often with high-quality data) whose metadata are not available and whose data are not readily accessible.
- Unofficial observers supplying data to the NWS (lack of access to current data and historic archives; lack of metadata).
- Networks having no available historic data.
- Networks having poor-quality metadata.
- Networks having poor access to metadata.
- Real-time networks having poor access to real-time data.

Previous inventory efforts at WRCC have shown that for the weather networks identified in the preceding list, in light of the need for quality data to track weather and climate, the resources required and difficulty encountered in obtaining metadata or data are prohibitively large.

## 3.2. Criteria for Locating Stations

To identify weather and climate stations for each park unit in the ROMN we selected only those stations located within 40 km of the ROMN park units. This buffer distance was selected in an attempt to include at least a few automated stations from major networks such as SAO, but also to keep the size of the stations lists to a reasonable number.

The station locator maps presented in Chapter 4 were designed to show clearly the spatial distributions of all major weather/climate station networks in ROMN. We recognize that other mapping formats may be more suitable for other specific needs.

# 4.0. Station Inventory

An objective of this report is to show the locations of weather/climate stations for the ROMN region in relation to the boundaries of the NPS park units within the ROMN. A station does not have to be within park boundaries to provide useful data and information for a park unit.

## 4.1. Climate and Weather Networks

Most stations in the ROMN region are associated with at least one of 23 major weather/climate networks (Table 4.1). Brief descriptions of each weather/climate network are provided below (see Appendix G for greater detail).

Table 4.1. Weather and climate networks represented within the ROMN.

| Acronym | Name |
| --- | --- |
| AgriMet | Pacific Northwest Cooperative Agricultural Network |
| BWFO | NWS Forecast Office, Boulder, Colorado |
| CANADA | Canadian weather/climate stations |
| CASTNet | Clean Air Status and Trends Network |
| CDOT | Colorado Department of Transportation network |
| CoAgMet | Colorado Agricultural Meteorological network |
| COOP | NWS Cooperative Observer Program |
| CRBFC | Colorado River Basin Forecast Center network |
| CWOP | Citizen Weather Observer Program |
| DUDFCD | Denver Urban Drainage and Flood Control District network |
| GNP | Glacier National Park network |
| GPMP | NPS Gaseous Pollutant Monitoring Program |
| GPS-MET | NOAA ground-based GPS meteorology network |
| LTER | U.S. Long Term Ecological Research network |
| MSOWFO | NWS Forecast Office, Missoula, Montana |
| MT DOT | Montana Department of Transportation network |
| NADP | National Atmospheric Deposition Program |
| NRCS-SC | NRCS snowcourse network |
| POMS | Portable Ozone Monitoring System |
| RAWS | Remote Automated Weather Station network |
| SAO | NWS/FAA Surface Airways Observation network |
| SNOTEL | USDA/NRCS Snowfall Telemetry network |
| WX4U | Weather For You network |

### 4.1.1. Pacific Northwest Cooperative Agricultural Network (AgriMet)

AgriMet is a network of automated weather stations operated by the U.S. Bureau of Reclamation. The stations in AgriMet are located primarily in irrigated agricultural areas throughout the Pacific Northwest.

### 4.1.2. NWS Forecast Office, Boulder, Colorado (BWFO)
These are near-real-time stations managed by the NWS forecast office in Boulder, Colorado. Data from these stations are used to provide local weather data to assist in developing routine weather forecasts for the northern Front Range of Colorado. Measured meteorological elements include temperature, precipitation, wind, and relative humidity.

### 4.1.3. Canadian Weather/Climate Stations (CANADA)
These include various automated weather/climate station networks from Canada. The Meteorological Service of Canada operates many of these stations, including airport sites. The data measured at these sites generally include temperature, precipitation, humidity, wind, pressure, sky cover, ceiling, visibility, and current weather. Most of the data records are of high quality.

### 4.1.4. Clean Air Status and Trends Network (CASTNet)
CASTNet is primarily an air-quality monitoring network managed by the EPA and the NPS Air Resources Division. Standard hourly weather and climate elements are measured and include temperature, wind, humidity, solar radiation, soil temperature, and sometimes moisture. These elements are intended to support interpretation of air-quality parameters that also are measured at CASTNet sites. Data records at CASTNet sites are generally one–two decades in length.

### 4.1.5. Colorado Department of Transportation (CDOT) Network
These weather stations are operated by CDOT in support of management activities for Colorado's transportation network. Measured meteorological elements include temperature, precipitation, wind, and relative humidity.

### 4.1.6. Colorado Agricultural Meteorological Network (CoAgMet)
The CoAgMet network is a weather monitoring network originally started in the early 1990s by the Agricultural Research Service branch of the USDA and the Plant Pathology extension service at Colorado State University. Data are managed by the Colorado Climate Center. Measured elements include temperature, precipitation, wind, relative humidity, solar radiation, and soil temperature.

### 4.1.7. NWS Cooperative Observer Program (COOP)
The COOP network has been a foundation of the U.S. climate program for decades and continues to play an important role. Manual measurements are made by volunteers and consist of daily maximum and minimum temperatures, observation-time temperature, daily precipitation, daily snowfall, and snow depth. When blended with NWS measurements, the data set is known as SOD, or "Summary of the Day." The quality of data from COOP sites ranges from excellent to modest.

### 4.1.8. Colorado River Basin Forecast Center (CRBFC) Network
The CRBFC network has over 100 weather stations in the Colorado River Basin. The primary purpose of CRBFC stations is to collect meteorological data in support of efforts by the CRBFC to monitor potential flood conditions in the Colorado River Basin.

### 4.1.9. Citizen Weather Observer Program (CWOP)

The CWOP network consists primarily of automated weather stations operated by private citizens who have either an Internet connection and/or a wireless Ham radio setup. Data from CWOP stations are specifically intended for use in research, education, and homeland security activities. Although standard meteorological elements such as temperature, precipitation, and wind are measured at all CWOP stations, station characteristics do vary, including sensor types and site exposure.

### 4.1.10. Denver Urban Drainage Flood Control District (DUDFCD) Network

The DUDFCD operates a set of weather stations whose primary purpose is to collect near-real-time precipitation measurements in support of efforts by the DUDFCD to manage and monitor potential flood conditions in the greater Denver area.

### 4.1.11. Glacier National Park Network (GNP)

The GNP network is a local network of weather/climate stations whose primary purpose is to provide local meteorological data for Glacier National Park (GLAC). These stations are primarily located along or near the Going-to-the-Sun Road.

### 4.1.12. Gaseous Pollutant Monitoring Program (GPMP)

The GPMP network measures hourly meteorological data in support of pollutant monitoring activities. Measured elements include temperature, precipitation, humidity, wind, solar radiation, and surface wetness. These data are generally of high quality, with records extending up to two decades in length.

### 4.1.13. NOAA Ground-Based GPS Meteorology (GPS-MET) Network

The GPS-MET network is the first network of its kind dedicated to GPS (Global Positioning System) meteorology (see Duan et al. 1996), which utilizes the radio signals broadcast by the satellite for atmospheric remote sensing. GPS meteorology applications have evolved along two paths: ground-based (Bevis et al. 1992) and space-based (Yuan et al. 1993). For more information, please see Appendix G. The stations identified in this inventory are all ground-based. The GPS-MET network was developed in response to the need for improved moisture observations to support weather forecasting, climate monitoring, and other research activities. The primary goals of this network are to measure atmospheric water vapor using ground-based GPS receivers, facilitate the operational use of these data, and encourage usage of GPS meteorology for atmospheric research and other applications. GPS-MET is a collaboration between NOAA and several other governmental and university organizations and institutions. Ancillary meteorological observations at GPS-MET stations include temperature, relative humidity, and pressure.

### 4.1.14. U.S. Long-Term Ecological Research (LTER) Network

This network, which started in 1980, is a collaborative effort among ecologists around the U.S. to investigate ecological processes over a wide range of spatial and temporal scales. Near-real-time climate elements are measured at LTER sites in support of ongoing ecological research efforts. The climate elements measured vary from site to site but generally include temperature, precipitation, wind, and relative humidity.

### 4.1.15. NWS Forecast Office, Missoula, Montana (MSOWFO)
These are near-real-time stations managed by the NWS forecast office in Missoula, Montana. Data from these stations are used to provide local weather data to assist in developing routine weather forecasts for western Montana. Measured meteorological elements include temperature, precipitation, wind, and relative humidity.

### 4.1.16. Montana Department of Transportation (MT DOT) Network
These weather stations are operated by MT DOT in support of management activities for Montana's transportation network. Measured meteorological elements include temperature, precipitation, wind, and relative humidity.

### 4.1.17. National Atmospheric Deposition Program (NADP)
The purpose of the NADP network is to monitor primarily wet deposition at selected sites around the U.S. and its territories. The network is a collaborative effort among several agencies including NPS, USDA and the U.S. Geological Survey (USGS). Precipitation is the primary climate parameter measured at NADP sites. This network includes stations from the Mercury Deposition Network (MDN).

### 4.1.18. USDA/NRCS Snowcourse Network (NRCS-SC)
The USDA/NRCS maintains a network of snow-monitoring stations in addition to SNOTEL (described below). These sites are known as snowcourses. These are all manual sites, measuring only snow depth and snow water content one–two times per month during the months of January to June. Data records for these snowcourses often extend back to the 1920s or 1930s, and the data are generally of high quality. Many of these sites have been replaced by SNOTEL sites, but several hundred snowcourses are still in operation.

### 4.1.19. Portable Ozone Monitoring System (POMS)
The POMS network is operated by the NPS Air Resources Division. Sites are intended primarily for summer, short-term (1-5 years) monitoring of near-surface atmospheric ozone levels in remote locations. Measured meteorological elements include temperature, precipitation, wind, relative humidity, and solar radiation.

### 4.1.20. Remote Automated Weather Station (RAWS) Network
The RAWS network is administered through many land management agencies, particularly the BLM and the Forest Service. Hourly meteorology elements are measured and include temperature, wind, humidity, solar radiation, barometric pressure, fuel temperature, and precipitation (when temperatures are above freezing). The fire community is the primary client for RAWS data. These sites are remote and data typically are transmitted via GOES (Geostationary Operational Environmental Satellite). Some sites operate all winter. Most data records for RAWS sites began during or after the mid-1980s.

### 4.1.21. NWS Surface Airways Observation Network (SAO)
These stations are located usually at major airports and military bases. Almost all SAO sites are automated. The hourly data measured at these sites include temperature, precipitation, humidity, wind, pressure, sky cover, ceiling, visibility, and current weather. Most data records begin during or after the 1940s, and these data are generally of high quality.

### 4.1.22. USDA/NRCS Snowfall Telemetry (SNOTEL) Network

The USDA/NRCS maintains a network of automated snow-monitoring stations known as SNOTEL. The network was implemented originally to measure daily precipitation and snow water content. Many modern SNOTEL sites now record hourly data, with some sites now recording temperature and snow depth. Most data records began during or after the mid-1970s.

### 4.1.23. Weather For You Network (WX4U)

The WX4U network is a nationwide collection of weather stations run by local observers. Data quality varies with site. Standard meteorological elements are measured and usually include temperature, precipitation, wind, and humidity.

### 4.1.24. Weather Bureau Army Navy (WBAN)

Some stations are identified in this report as WBAN stations. This is a station identification system rather than a true weather/climate network. Stations identified with WBAN are largely historical stations that reported meteorological observations on the WBAN weather observation forms that were common during the early and middle parts of the twentieth century. The use of WBAN numbers to identify stations was one of the first attempts in the U.S. to use a coordinated station numbering scheme between several weather station networks, such as the COOP and SAO networks.

### 4.1.25. Other Networks

In addition to the major networks mentioned above, there are various networks that are operated for specific purposes by specific organizations or governmental agencies or scientific research projects. These networks could be present within ROMN but have not been identified in this report. Some of the commonly used networks include the following:

- NOAA upper-air stations
- Federal and state departments of transportation
- U.S. Department of Energy Surface Radiation Budget Network (Surfrad)
- Park-specific-monitoring networks and stations
- Other research or project networks having many possible owners

## 4.2. Station Locations

The major weather/climate networks in the ROMN (discussed in Section 4.1) have at most about a dozen stations at or inside each park unit (Table 4.2). Most of these are COOP stations.

Lists of stations have been compiled for the ROMN. As was previously mentioned, a station does not have to be within the boundaries to provide useful data and information regarding the park unit in question. Some might be physically *within* the administrative or political boundaries, whereas others might be just outside, or even some distance away, but would be "*nearby*" in terms of behavior and representativeness. What constitutes "useful" and "representative" are also significant questions, whose answers can vary according to application, type of element, period of record, procedural or methodological observation conventions, and the like.

Table 4.2. Number of stations within or nearby ROMN park units. Numbers are listed by park unit and by weather/climate network. Figures in parentheses indicate the numbers of stations within park boundaries.

| Network | FLFO | GLAC | GRKO | GRSA | LIBI | ROMO |
|---|---|---|---|---|---|---|
| AgriMet | 0(0) | 1(0) | 1(0) | 0(0) | 0(0) | 0(0) |
| BWFO | 1(0) | 0(0) | 0(0) | 0(0) | 0(0) | 11(0) |
| CANADA | 0(0) | 1(0) | 0(0) | 0(0) | 0(0) | 0(0) |
| CASTNet | 0(0) | 1(1) | 0(0) | 0(0) | 0(0) | 1(0) |
| CDOT | 11(0) | 0(0) | 0(0) | 1(0) | 0(0) | 6(0) |
| CoAgMet | 0(0) | 0(0) | 0(0) | 3(0) | 0(0) | 1(0) |
| COOP | 22(1) | 42(14) | 16(0) | 20(1) | 7(0) | 63(2) |
| CRBFC | 0(0) | 0(0) | 0(0) | 0(0) | 0(0) | 3(1) |
| CWOP | 17(0) | 1(0) | 0(0) | 1(0) | 2(0) | 29(0) |
| DUDFCD | 0(0) | 0(0) | 0(0) | 0(0) | 0(0) | 6(0) |
| GNP | 0(0) | 3(3) | 0(0) | 0(0) | 0(0) | 0(0) |
| GPMP | 0(0) | 0(0) | 0(0) | 1(1) | 0(0) | 1(0) |
| GPS-MET | 0(0) | 0(0) | 0(0) | 0(0) | 0(0) | 5(0) |
| LTER | 0(0) | 0(0) | 0(0) | 0(0) | 0(0) | 10(0) |
| MSOWFO | 0(0) | 5(1) | 0(0) | 0(0) | 0(0) | 0(0) |
| MT DOT | 0(0) | 4(0) | 3(0) | 0(0) | 0(0) | 0(0) |
| NADP | 1(0) | 2(1) | 1(0) | 1(0) | 1(1) | 5(2) |
| NRCS-SC | 1(0) | 36(8) | 13(0) | 3(0) | 0(0) | 28(7) |
| POMS | 0(0) | 0(0) | 0(0) | 0(0) | 0(0) | 1(0) |
| RAWS | 9(0) | 13(3) | 1(0) | 6(1) | 2(1) | 7(1) |
| SAO | 1(0) | 1(0) | 2(0) | 3(0) | 1(0) | 3(0) |
| SNOTEL | 0(0) | 8(2) | 2(0) | 2(1) | 0(0) | 13(5) |
| WX4U | 0(0) | 0(0) | 0(0) | 1(0) | 0(0) | 1(0) |
| Other | 1(0) | 0(0) | 2(0) | 2(0) | 2(0) | 4(0) |
| Total | 64(1) | 118(33) | 41(0) | 44(4) | 15(2) | 198(18) |

### 4.2.1. Glacier National Park

We identified 33 weather/climate stations within the boundaries of GLAC (Table 4.3; Figure 4.1). All but six of these stations are active. Stations from at least eight different weather or climate networks are currently operating within the park unit. However, most of these stations are either COOP or NRCS-SC stations. In addition to these manual stations, a NADP station is operating at West Glacier ("Glacier NP;" 2003-present).

Of the 14 COOP stations identified within GLAC, eight are active (Table 4.3). The longest record we identified among these active climate stations was from the COOP station "West Glacier," at the west entrance of GLAC. This climate station has been active since 1948 and its data record is very complete. A few other COOP stations in the park unit have data records going back to the 1950s, including "Belly River RS" (1956-present) in northeastern GLAC, "Polebridge RS" (1953-present) in northwestern GLAC, and "St. Mary RS" (1953-present) near the east entrance of GLAC.

Glacier National Park operates a small network (GNP) of three stations within the park unit (Table 4.3; Figure 4.1). Two of these stations, "Garden Wall" and "Logan Pass Visitors Center," are located in central GLAC. "Snowslip" is a GNP station in extreme southern GLAC, near U.S. Highway 2.

Table 4.3. Weather and climate stations for Glacier National Park (GLAC). Stations inside GLAC and within 40 km of GLAC are included. Missing entries are indicated by "M".

## Glacier National Park (GLAC)

| Name | Lat. | Lon. | Elev. (m) | Network | Start | End | In Park? |
|------|------|------|-----------|---------|-------|-----|----------|
| Glacier NP | 48.510 | -113.996 | 976 | CASTNet | 1/1/1992 | Present | Yes |
| Belly River RS | 48.933 | -113.717 | 1403 | COOP | 7/1/1956 | Present | Yes |
| Essex Highway 2 Bridge | 48.275 | -113.603 | 1136 | COOP | 4/1/1976 | Present | Yes |
| Grinnell Glacier #1 | 48.767 | -113.717 | 1903 | COOP | 8/1/1949 | 8/31/1974 | Yes |
| Grinnell Glacier #2 | 48.750 | -113.717 | 1870 | COOP | 8/1/1955 | 7/31/1971 | Yes |
| Many Glacier | 48.800 | -113.650 | 1491 | COOP | 8/1/1967 | 3/31/1981 | Yes |
| Mount Brown Lookout | 48.633 | -113.833 | 2349 | COOP | 7/1/1953 | 12/31/1958 | Yes |
| Polebridge Flathead | 48.783 | -114.282 | 1077 | COOP | 8/1/1980 | Present | Yes |
| Polebridge RS | 48.783 | -114.267 | 1083 | COOP | 7/1/1954 | Present | Yes |
| Saint Mary 1 SSW | 48.741 | -113.433 | 1388 | COOP | 9/25/2003 | Present | Yes |
| Sperry Chalet | 48.617 | -113.783 | 2059 | COOP | 6/1/1960 | 12/31/1978 | Yes |
| St. Mary | 48.738 | -113.429 | 1390 | COOP | 5/1/1981 | Present | Yes |
| St. Mary RS | 48.733 | -113.433 | 1373 | COOP | 6/1/1953 | Present | Yes |
| West Glacier | 48.500 | -113.985 | 961 | COOP | 7/1/1948 | Present | Yes |
| West Glacier 1 W | 48.500 | -114.017 | 955 | COOP | 4/1/1952 | 6/1/1987 | Yes |
| Garden Wall | 48.742 | -113.737 | 2256 | GNP | M | Present | Yes |
| Logan Pass Visitors Center | 48.695 | -113.717 | 2065 | GNP | M | Present | Yes |
| Snowslip | 48.255 | -113.502 | 2140 | GNP | M | Present | Yes |
| Garden Wall USGS | 48.730 | -113.730 | 2240 | MSOWFO | M | Present | Yes |
| Glacier NP | 48.510 | -113.996 | 980 | NADP | 10/28/2003 | Present | Yes |
| Iceberg Lake No. 3 | 48.833 | -113.717 | 1707 | NRCS-SC | 1/1/1922 | Present | Yes |
| Josephine Lower No. 9 | 48.783 | -113.667 | 1494 | NRCS-SC | 1/1/1955 | Present | Yes |
| Kishenehn | 48.967 | -114.417 | 1186 | NRCS-SC | 1/1/1946 | Present | Yes |
| Many Glacier | 48.800 | -113.667 | 1494 | NRCS-SC | 1/1/1977 | Present | Yes |
| Mineral Creek | 48.767 | -113.817 | 1219 | NRCS-SC | 1/1/1939 | Present | Yes |
| Mount Allen No. 7 | 48.767 | -113.683 | 1737 | NRCS-SC | 1/1/1922 | Present | Yes |
| Piegan Pass No. 6 | 48.767 | -113.700 | 1676 | NRCS-SC | 1/1/1922 | Present | Yes |
| Ptarmigan No 8 | 48.833 | -113.717 | 1768 | NRCS-SC | 1/1/1937 | Present | Yes |
| Polebridge | 48.783 | -114.280 | 1067 | RAWS | 7/1/2003 | Present | Yes |
| St. Mary | 48.738 | -113.431 | 1390 | RAWS | 1/1/1986 | Present | Yes |
| West Glacier | 48.511 | -113.994 | 975 | RAWS | 6/1/2001 | Present | Yes |
| Flattop Mtn. | 48.800 | -113.850 | 1920 | SNOTEL | 1/1/1970 | Present | Yes |
| Many Glacier | 48.800 | -113.667 | 1494 | SNOTEL | 10/1/1976 | Present | Yes |
| Creston | 48.188 | -114.128 | 899 | Agrimet | 6/1/2001 | 12/31/2001 | No |
| Cardston Automated Reporting | 49.200 | -113.283 | 1136 | CANADA | M | Present | No |
| Babb 6 NE | 48.939 | -113.372 | 1311 | COOP | 5/15/1906 | Present | No |
| Browning | 48.559 | -113.011 | 1327 | COOP | 5/14/1894 | Present | No |
| Browning No. 2 | 48.550 | -113.017 | 1335 | COOP | 1/9/1990 | 1/2/1997 | No |
| Columbia Falls | 48.367 | -114.183 | 909 | COOP | 7/1/1948 | 7/21/1983 | No |

## Glacier National Park (GLAC)

| Name | Lat. | Lon. | Elev. (m) | Network | Start | End | In Park? |
|---|---|---|---|---|---|---|---|
| Columbia Falls 5 SW | 48.317 | -114.200 | 939 | COOP | 3/1/1893 | 6/30/1949 | No |
| Columbia Falls RS | 48.367 | -114.183 | 915 | COOP | 1/1/1949 | 9/30/1950 | No |
| Coram RS | 48.400 | -114.017 | 976 | COOP | 5/1/1953 | 10/31/1957 | No |
| Creston | 48.189 | -114.134 | 896 | COOP | 2/1/1949 | Present | No |
| Desert Mountain Look | 48.433 | -113.967 | 1943 | COOP | 7/1/1953 | Present | No |
| East Glacier | 48.447 | -113.224 | 1465 | COOP | 8/1/1949 | Present | No |
| Essex | 48.283 | -113.606 | 1173 | COOP | 8/1/1951 | Present | No |
| Fortine 1 N | 48.778 | -114.900 | 914 | COOP | 3/1/1906 | Present | No |
| Heart Butte | 48.293 | -112.835 | 1373 | COOP | 5/1/1949 | Present | No |
| Hungry Horse Dam | 48.343 | -114.022 | 963 | COOP | 6/1/1947 | Present | No |
| Hungry Horse RS | 48.383 | -114.050 | 955 | COOP | 5/1/1958 | Present | No |
| Kalispell | 48.189 | -114.311 | 896 | COOP | 6/1/1896 | 7/1/2006 | No |
| Kalispell 9 NNE | 48.307 | -114.246 | 905 | COOP | 12/20/1996 | 9/13/2005 | No |
| Olney | 48.550 | -114.574 | 965 | COOP | 5/1/1962 | Present | No |
| Polebridge | 48.765 | -114.284 | 1073 | COOP | 7/6/1933 | Present | No |
| Red Plume Lookout | 48.150 | -113.300 | 2437 | COOP | 7/1/1956 | Present | No |
| Sherburne Lake | 48.833 | -113.517 | 1495 | COOP | 9/1/1932 | 9/30/1952 | No |
| Spotted Bear Lookout | 47.900 | -113.433 | 2205 | COOP | 7/1/1953 | Present | No |
| Spotted Bear Mtn. | 47.917 | -113.467 | 1830 | COOP | 8/1/1948 | 9/30/1976 | No |
| Spotted Bear RS | 47.917 | -113.517 | 1138 | COOP | 7/1/1953 | 7/20/1961 | No |
| Summit | 48.316 | -113.354 | 1595 | COOP | 1/1/1903 | Present | No |
| Swift Dam | 48.164 | -112.867 | 1457 | COOP | 4/1/1965 | Present | No |
| Upper Columbia Stn. L. | 48.300 | -113.367 | 1479 | COOP | 7/1/1948 | 6/30/1951 | No |
| Whitefish | 48.408 | -114.359 | 945 | COOP | 11/1/1939 | Present | No |
| CW1603 Kalispell | 48.305 | -114.434 | 969 | CWOP | M | Present | No |
| Columbia Falls | 48.360 | -114.140 | 945 | MSOWFO | M | Present | No |
| Kalispell Downtown | 48.190 | -114.310 | 898 | MSOWFO | M | Present | No |
| North Fork Flathead | 48.500 | -114.130 | 959 | MSOWFO | M | Present | No |
| Olney | 48.550 | -114.570 | 965 | MSOWFO | M | Present | No |
| Dickey Lake US-93 MP 160.2 | 48.695 | -114.784 | 1063 | MT DOT | M | Present | No |
| Essex US-2 MP 179.9 | 48.282 | -113.607 | 1173 | MT DOT | M | Present | No |
| Flathead River MT 35 MP49 | 48.219 | -114.238 | 869 | MT DOT | M | Present | No |
| Two Medicine Brdg US-2 MP 210 | 48.453 | -113.195 | 1448 | MT DOT | M | Present | No |
| Glacier NP-St Mary RS | 48.741 | -113.430 | 1391 | NADP | 1/25/1983 | 11/28/1989 | No |
| Akamina | 49.000 | -114.050 | 1800 | NRCS-SC | M | Present | No |
| Badger Pass | 48.133 | -113.017 | 2103 | NRCS-SC | 1/1/1964 | Present | No |
| Blue Lake | 48.150 | -113.100 | 1798 | NRCS-SC | 1/1/1969 | Present | No |
| Camp Misery | 48.167 | -113.933 | 1951 | NRCS-SC | 1/1/1962 | Present | No |
| Chicken Creek | 48.617 | -114.517 | 1237 | NRCS-SC | 1/1/1978 | Present | No |
| Desert Mountain | 48.417 | -113.950 | 1707 | NRCS-SC | 1/1/1937 | Present | No |

## Glacier National Park (GLAC)

| Name | Lat. | Lon. | Elev. (m) | Network | Start | End | In Park? |
|---|---|---|---|---|---|---|---|
| Emery Creek | 48.433 | -113.933 | 1326 | NRCS-SC | 1/1/1976 | Present | No |
| Gardiner Headwaters | 49.350 | -114.017 | 1970 | NRCS-SC | M | Present | No |
| Grave Creek | 48.917 | -114.767 | 1311 | NRCS-SC | 1/1/1965 | Present | No |
| Gunsight Lake | 47.983 | -113.333 | 1920 | NRCS-SC | 1/1/1964 | Present | No |
| Hell Roaring Divide | 48.500 | -114.350 | 1759 | NRCS-SC | 1/1/1942 | Present | No |
| Herrig Junction | 48.700 | -114.617 | 1478 | NRCS-SC | 1/1/1977 | Present | No |
| Lee Creek Site D | 49.017 | -113.617 | 1660 | NRCS-SC | M | Present | No |
| Lee Creek Site E | 49.017 | -113.650 | 1675 | NRCS-SC | M | Present | No |
| Lee Creek Site F | 49.050 | -113.483 | 1570 | NRCS-SC | M | Present | No |
| Lee Creek Site P | 49.033 | -113.567 | 1525 | NRCS-SC | M | Present | No |
| Lee Creek Site Q | 49.050 | -113.600 | 1500 | NRCS-SC | M | Present | No |
| Marias Pass | 48.317 | -113.350 | 1600 | NRCS-SC | 1/1/1934 | Present | No |
| Middle Drywood | 49.250 | -114.050 | 1570 | NRCS-SC | M | Present | No |
| Noisy Basin | 48.150 | -113.950 | 1841 | NRCS-SC | 1/1/1975 | Present | No |
| Pike Creek | 48.300 | -113.333 | 1807 | NRCS-SC | 1/1/1977 | Present | No |
| Spotted Bear Mountain | 47.900 | -113.450 | 2134 | NRCS-SC | 1/1/1948 | Present | No |
| Stahl Peak | 48.917 | -114.867 | 1838 | NRCS-SC | 1/1/1969 | Present | No |
| Stryker Basin | 48.683 | -114.650 | 1884 | NRCS-SC | 1/1/1977 | Present | No |
| Trinkus Lake | 47.950 | -113.750 | 1859 | NRCS-SC | 1/1/1949 | Present | No |
| Twin Creeks | 47.983 | -113.567 | 1091 | NRCS-SC | 1/1/1951 | Present | No |
| W.Castle (Bush) | 49.317 | -114.400 | 1520 | NRCS-SC | M | Present | No |
| Weasel Divide | 48.950 | -114.733 | 1661 | NRCS-SC | 1/1/1937 | Present | No |
| Badger Pass | 48.167 | -113.000 | 2103 | RAWS | 6/1/1992 | Present | No |
| Big Mountain | 48.502 | -114.339 | 2078 | RAWS | 12/14/1992 | 12/19/1993 | No |
| Browning BFA | 48.562 | -113.013 | 1336 | RAWS | 10/1/2003 | Present | No |
| Cyclone | 48.716 | -114.336 | 1615 | RAWS | 8/1/1986 | Present | No |
| Deep Creek BFA | 48.356 | -113.114 | 1628 | RAWS | 10/1/2003 | Present | No |
| Fielding | 48.278 | -113.436 | 1402 | RAWS | 9/1/2004 | Present | No |
| Heart Butte | 48.293 | -112.835 | 1353 | RAWS | 12/1/2004 | Present | No |
| Hungry Horse | 48.385 | -114.058 | 983 | RAWS | 5/1/1999 | Present | No |
| Spotted Bear | 47.904 | -113.439 | 2202 | RAWS | 10/1/1990 | Present | No |
| Stillwater | 48.539 | -114.559 | 950 | RAWS | 7/1/2002 | Present | No |
| Kalispell | 48.304 | -114.264 | 901 | SAO | 6/1/1896 | Present | No |
| Badger Pass | 48.133 | -113.017 | 2103 | SNOTEL | 10/1/1978 | Present | No |
| Emery Creek | 48.433 | -113.933 | 1326 | SNOTEL | 10/1/1976 | Present | No |
| Grave Creek | 48.917 | -114.767 | 1311 | SNOTEL | 10/1/1975 | Present | No |
| Noisy Basion | 48.150 | -113.950 | 1841 | SNOTEL | M | Present | No |
| Pike Creek Montana | 48.300 | -113.333 | 1807 | SNOTEL | M | Present | No |
| Stahl Peak | 48.917 | -114.867 | 1838 | SNOTEL | 10/1/1975 | Present | No |

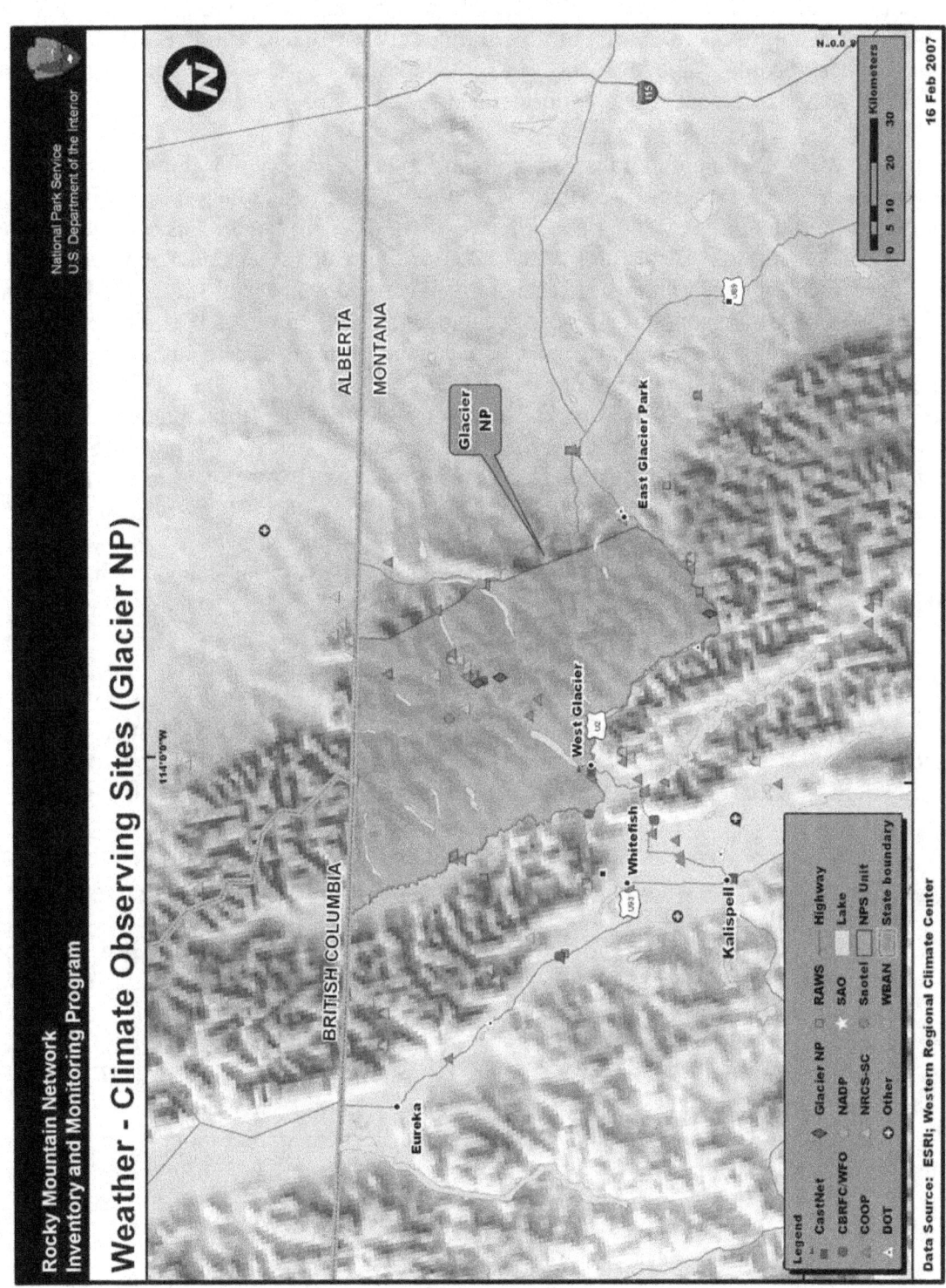

Figure 4.1. Station locations for Glacier National Park.

In addition to the three GNP stations discussed previously, several networks provide near-real-time weather data within GLAC. The CASTNet station "Glacier NP" has been operating since 1992 (Table 4.3) near the west entrance of GLAC (Figure 4.1). The Missoula NWS weather forecast office (MSOWFO) operates a weather station in central GLAC (Garden Wall USGS). Three active RAWS weather stations were identified within GLAC, two at the east and west entrances of the park unit ("St. Mary" and "West Glacier," respectively) and the third (Polebridge) in the northwestern portion of the park unit. "West Glacier" and "Polebridge" have very complete data records, while "St. Mary" has one gap from February through April of 1996. Two SNOTEL stations were identified in northern/eastern GLAC.

We identified 28 COOP climate stations within 40 km of GLAC (Table 4.3). Seventeen of these climate stations are active currently. The longest record we identified among these active stations was from the COOP station "Browning," 24 km east of GLAC. This station has been active since 1894 and its data record was reliable until 1989. After this time, numerous data gaps have occurred. The COOP station "Summit" is just south of GLAC on U.S. Highway 2 and has been active since 1903. Its data record has not been reliable since 1979. The COOP station "Babb 6 NE" is 17 km northeast of GLAC and has been active since 1906. Its data record has been quite reliable except for no weekend observations in the 1970s and since 1995. The COOP station "Fortine 1 N" is 40 km west of GLAC and has been active since 1906. Its data record was quite reliable until the late 1980s. After this, numerous data gaps have occurred. "Polebridge" is a COOP station just northwest of GLAC that has been active since 1933. Its data record has been unreliable since 2000. The COOP station "Whitefish" (1939-present) is 20 km west of GLAC. This station has had reliable data since 1987. A large data gap occurred between July 1983 and May 1987. Before 1983, this station measured precipitation only. Other manual sites within 40 km of the boundaries of GRSA include the NADP station "Glacier NP-St. Mary RS," which operated between 1983 and 1989, and numerous NRCS-SC sites.

The Missoula NWS weather forecast office (MSOWFO) operates four weather stations within 40 km of GLAC (Table 4.3). These are all south and west of GLAC. Four MT DOT stations were identified within 40 km of GLAC. Two of these are along U.S. Highway 2 (Figure 4.1), one is along U.S. Highway 93 (west of GLAC), and one is along State Highway 35 (south of GLAC).

Ten RAWS stations were identified within 40 km of GLAC boundaries (Table 4.3). Nine of these weather stations are active currently. The most reliable records are at the RAWS stations "Browning BFA" (2003-present), 24 km east of GLAC (Figure 4.1); "Deep Creek BFA" (2003-present), 11 km southeast of GLAC; and "Fielding" (2004-present), just south of GLAC. The RAWS station "Badger Pass" is unreliable. It is located 32 km southeast of GLAC. Three RAWS stations (Heart Butte, Hungry Horse, and Stillwater) have only provided reliable data in the past 1-3 years, despite having longer data records. "Heart Butte" is 33 km southeast of GLAC, "Hungry Horse" is 9 km southwest of GLAC, and "Stillwater" is 31 km west of GLAC. The RAWS stations "Cyclone" (1986-present; 6 km west of GLAC) and "Spotted Bear" (1990-present; 38 km south of GLAC) only take observations during the summer months (June-September, generally).

The SAO station "Kalispell" is the only SAO station we identified within 40 km of GLAC. This station has been operating since 1896 and is 23 km southwest of GLAC.

Six SNOTEL stations were identified within 40 km of GLAC. Two of these ("Grave Creek" and "Stahl Peak") are west of the park unit, while the remaining stations are south and east of the park unit.

### 4.2.2. Grant-Kohrs Ranch National Historic Site

No weather or climate stations were identified within GRKO (Table 4.4). The MT DOT operates three automated weather stations, mostly north and east of the park unit (Figure 4.2). Numerous NRCS-SC stations were identified within 40 km of GRKO, mostly in the mountain ranges surrounding the park unit. Two SAO stations with long-term data records were identified within 40 km of GRKO. "Drummond" (1927-present) is 40 km northwest of GRKO, while "Elliston" (1909-present) is 27 km northeast of GRKO. Two SNOTEL stations were identified within 40 km of GRKO. "Rocker Peak" (1970-present) is 37 km east of GRKO, while "Warm Springs" (1977-present) is 34 km southwest of GRKO.

We identified 16 COOP stations within 40 km of GRKO (Table 4.4). Five of these climate stations are shown to be currently active and three of these are located in the vicinity of Deer Lodge. Three of the active stations (Anaconda, Deer Lodge 2, and Drummond) are listed as having long-term records. However, in each case, there is sufficient evidence to believe that these records are comprised of two or more separate records from different stations.

### 4.2.3. Little Bighorn Battlefield National Monument

Two stations were identified within the boundaries of LIBI (Table 4.4). One of these is a NADP station, "Little Bighorn Battlefield NM," which has been operating since 1984. The other station is a RAWS weather station, "Little Bighorn," which has been operating since 1997. The data record at this RAWS site shows a gap in August and September of 2006.

Seven COOP stations were identified within 40 km of the boundaries of LIBI. Three of these are active currently (Table 4.4). The longest record we identified among these active stations was from the COOP station "Lodge Grass," 22 km south of LIBI. This climate station has been active since 1904; however, its data record is unreliable. A more reliable long-term record is at the COOP station "Busby," 32 km east of LIBI. This station has been active since 1907 and its data record is largely complete, with scattered, small data gaps. The COOP station "Hardin" is 22 km northwest of LIBI. With the exception of unreliable data during the 1970s and early 1980s, this station has a reliable data record (1948-present).

Besides the RAWS station within LIBI (Little Bighorn), we have identified four weather stations that provide near-real-time data within 40 km of the park unit (Table 4.4). CWOP stations are present in Hardin, 22 km northwest of LIBI, and Fort Smith, 35 km southwest of LIBI. The RAWS station "Wolf Mountain" is 28 km southeast of LIBI and has a very complete record going back to 1985. The SAO station "Lodge Grass," collocated with the COOP station of the same name, also provides near-real-time data.

Table 4.4. Weather and climate stations for the ROMN park units in southern Montana. Stations inside park units and within 40 km of the park unit boundary are included. Missing entries are indicated by "M".

| Name | Lat. | Lon. | Elev. (m) | Network | Start | End | In Park? |
|---|---|---|---|---|---|---|---|
| **Grant-Kohrs Ranch National Historic Site (GRKO)** | | | | | | | |
| Deer Lodge | 46.336 | -112.767 | 1426 | Agrimet | 6/1/2001 | 12/31/2001 | No |
| Anaconda | 46.131 | -112.957 | 1609 | COOP | 6/1/1894 | Present | No |
| Basin | 46.267 | -112.267 | 1641 | COOP | 10/31/1944 | 2/12/1971 | No |
| Basin 16 WSW | 46.233 | -112.583 | 2166 | COOP | 8/1/1949 | 8/31/1976 | No |
| Basin 3 W | 46.283 | -112.300 | 1687 | COOP | 2/1/1971 | 1/1/1973 | No |
| Deer Lodge 2 | 46.383 | -112.733 | 1382 | COOP | 1/1/1893 | Present | No |
| Deer Lodge 3 W | 46.391 | -112.798 | 1478 | COOP | 4/1/1959 | Present | No |
| Deer Lodge Clark | 46.398 | -112.742 | 1372 | COOP | 3/25/1994 | Present | No |
| Drummond | 46.638 | -113.176 | 1219 | COOP | 5/1/1927 | Present | No |
| Drummond 1 SSW | 46.667 | -113.133 | 1202 | COOP | 1/1/1931 | 5/31/1936 | No |
| East Anaconda | 46.100 | -112.917 | 1681 | COOP | 9/1/1905 | 7/28/1980 | No |
| East Anaconda 2 | 46.117 | -112.933 | 1585 | COOP | 7/1/1980 | 4/30/1982 | No |
| Macdonald Pass | 46.567 | -112.300 | 1909 | COOP | 5/1/1978 | 4/30/1980 | No |
| Mc Donald Pass 2 N | 46.583 | -112.300 | 2211 | COOP | 1/1/1960 | 3/31/1962 | No |
| Moulton Reservoir | 46.083 | -112.500 | 2042 | COOP | 6/1/1980 | 10/28/1986 | No |
| Rimini | 46.500 | -112.250 | 1585 | COOP | 10/13/1982 | 8/9/1984 | No |
| Warm Springs Creek | 46.183 | -112.750 | 1479 | COOP | 7/1/1909 | 12/31/1912 | No |
| Avon North MT-141 MP 8.1 | 46.697 | -112.659 | 1550 | MT DOT | M | Present | No |
| Garrison I-90 MP 174.4 | 46.524 | -112.808 | 1319 | MT DOT | M | Present | No |
| MacDonald Pass US-12 MP 27.9 | 46.561 | -112.309 | 1928 | MT DOT | M | Present | No |
| Clancy | 46.485 | -112.065 | 1448 | NADP | 1/24/1984 | Present | No |
| Black Mountain | 46.317 | -112.567 | 2362 | NRCS-SC | 1/1/1976 | Present | No |
| Cottonwood Creek | 46.367 | -112.567 | 1951 | NRCS-SC | 1/1/1974 | Present | No |
| Discovery Basin | 46.250 | -113.233 | 2149 | NRCS-SC | 1/1/1975 | Present | No |
| Dix Hill | 46.700 | -112.550 | 1951 | NRCS-SC | 1/1/1974 | Present | No |
| El Dorado Mine | 46.433 | -113.067 | 2377 | NRCS-SC | 1/1/1949 | Present | No |
| Fred Burr Pass | 46.300 | -113.167 | 2438 | NRCS-SC | 1/1/1957 | Present | No |
| Gold Creek Lake | 46.450 | -113.067 | 2195 | NRCS-SC | 1/1/1949 | Present | No |
| Moulton Reservoir | 46.083 | -112.500 | 2088 | NRCS-SC | 1/1/1976 | Present | No |
| Ophir Park | 46.717 | -112.533 | 2179 | NRCS-SC | 1/1/1974 | Present | No |
| Rocker Peak | 46.367 | -112.250 | 2438 | NRCS-SC | 1/1/1968 | Present | No |
| Ten Mile Lower | 46.450 | -112.283 | 2012 | NRCS-SC | 1/1/1935 | Present | No |
| Ten Mile Middle | 46.433 | -112.300 | 2073 | NRCS-SC | 1/1/1934 | Present | No |
| Warm Springs | 46.267 | -113.167 | 2377 | NRCS-SC | 1/1/1978 | Present | No |
| Phillipsburg | 46.317 | -113.300 | 1609 | RAWS | 5/1/2001 | Present | No |
| Drummond | 46.638 | -113.176 | 1219 | SAO | 5/1/1927 | Present | No |
| Elliston | 46.563 | -112.434 | 1548 | SAO | 7/1/1909 | Present | No |
| Rocker Peak | 46.367 | -112.250 | 2438 | SNOTEL | 1/1/1970 | Present | No |
| Warm Springs | 46.267 | -113.167 | 2377 | SNOTEL | 10/1/1977 | Present | No |
| Elliston | 46.567 | -112.433 | 547 | WBAN | M | Present | No |
| Warm Springs | 46.183 | -112.750 | 1479 | WBAN | 2/1/1940 | 9/30/1956 | No |
| **Little Bighorn Battlefield National Monument (LIBI)** | | | | | | | |

| Name | Lat. | Lon. | Elev. (m) | Network | Start | End | In Park? |
|---|---|---|---|---|---|---|---|
| Little Bighorn Battlefield NM | 45.569 | -107.438 | 957 | NADP | 7/13/1984 | Present | Yes |
| Little Bighorn | 45.570 | -107.436 | 1036 | RAWS | 7/1/1997 | Present | Yes |
| Busby | 45.540 | -106.960 | 1045 | COOP | 5/1/1907 | Present | No |
| Campbell Farm Camp 4 | 45.417 | -107.900 | 1113 | COOP | 2/17/1882 | 11/30/1962 | No |
| Crow Agency | 45.600 | -107.450 | 924 | COOP | 4/1/1898 | 8/1/1991 | No |
| Hardin | 45.732 | -107.608 | 885 | COOP | 7/1/1948 | Present | No |
| Hardin 3 E | 45.736 | -107.557 | 850 | COOP | 5/1/1971 | 4/18/2002 | No |
| Kirby 1 S | 45.317 | -106.983 | 1205 | COOP | 11/1/1959 | 12/2/1975 | No |
| Lodge Grass | 45.316 | -107.359 | 1024 | COOP | 4/1/1904 | Present | No |
| CW2427 Hardin | 45.726 | -107.608 | 887 | CWOP | M | Present | No |
| KI0BJ-2 Fort Smith | 45.378 | -107.798 | 944 | CWOP | M | Present | No |
| Wolf Mountain | 45.313 | -107.172 | 1590 | RAWS | 5/1/1985 | Present | No |
| Lodge Grass | 45.316 | -107.359 | 1024 | SAO | 4/1/1904 | Present | No |
| Hardin A. | 45.717 | -107.567 | 885 | WBAN | 9/1/1934 | 11/30/1939 | No |
| St. Xavier | 45.467 | -107.750 | 976 | WBAN | 4/1/1940 | 3/31/1942 | No |

### 4.2.4. Rocky Mountain National Park

We identified 18 weather and climate stations within the boundaries of ROMO (Table 4.5; Figure 4.3). All of these stations are active except the COOP station "Hidden Valley," which operated in northern ROMO from 1967 to 1974. Most of the stations within ROMO are either NRCS-SC sites or SNOTEL sites. Many of these stations, in turn, are concentrated either in the northwestern or southeastern portions of the park unit. The longest record we identified was at the COOP station "Grand Lake 1 NW," in southwestern ROMO. This climate station has been active since 1907 and its data record is very reliable. Two NADP stations currently operate within ROMO. "Rocky Mountain NP-Beaver" (1980-present) is in eastern ROMO, while "Rocky Mountain NP-Loch Vale" (1983-present) is in southcentral ROMO. The only RAWS station we identified within ROMO is "Harbison Meadow," located in southwestern ROMO. This site has been operating since 2003. The primary sources of automated data in ROMO include this RAWS station along with a CBRFC weather station near Grand Lake and the six SNOTEL sites mentioned previously.

The NWS weather forecast office in Boulder (BWFO) operates at least 11 automated stations within 40 km of ROMO (Table 4.5). Most of these are in the urban areas near Boulder and Denver, south and east of ROMO. However, the BWFO network also includes two weather stations in Fort Collins ("CSU Campus" and "CSU Foothills Campus"), northeast of ROMO. In a similar manner, the six CDOT stations and numerous CWOP stations identified for ROMO are generally located east of ROMO, along the Front Range.

We identified 61 COOP stations within 40 km of the boundaries of ROMO. Of these stations, 27 are active currently (Table 4.5). The longest record we identified among these active stations was from the COOP station "Boulder," 32 km southeast of ROMO. This station's data record is largely complete but has occasional larger data gaps. The most recent gap occurred from January to April of 1999. The COOP station "Waterdale" is 24 km east of ROMO and has been active

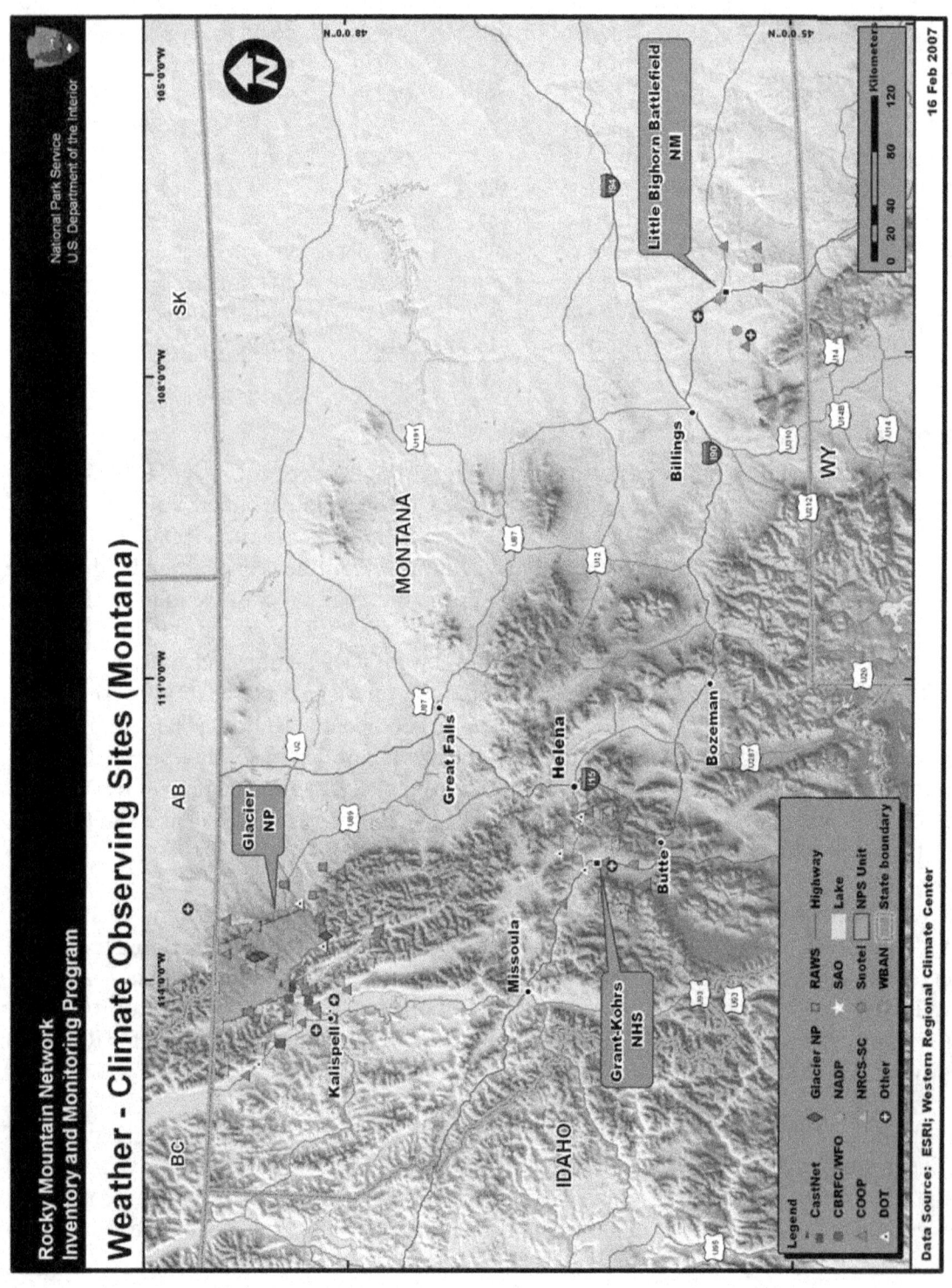

Figure 4.2. Station locations for the ROMN park units in Montana.

40

Table 4.5. Weather/climate stations for Rocky Mountain National Park (ROMO). Stations inside ROMO and within 40 km of ROMO are included. Missing entries are indicated by "M".

## Rocky Mountain National Park (ROMO)

| Name | Lat. | Lon. | Elev. (m) | Network | Start | End | In Park? |
|------|------|------|-----------|---------|-------|-----|----------|
| Grand Lake 1 NW | 40.267 | -105.832 | 2658 | COOP | 10/1/1907 | Present | Yes |
| Hidden Valley | 40.383 | -105.633 | 2751 | COOP | 9/1/1967 | 7/31/1974 | Yes |
| Grand Lake 1 NW | 40.267 | -105.832 | 2658 | CRBFC | M | Present | Yes |
| Rocky Mountain NP-Beaver | 40.364 | -105.581 | 2490 | NADP | 5/29/1980 | Present | Yes |
| Rocky Mountain NP-Loch Vale | 40.288 | -105.663 | 3159 | NADP | 8/16/1983 | Present | Yes |
| Deer Ridge | 40.400 | -105.633 | 2743 | NRCS-SC | 1/1/1949 | Present | Yes |
| Hidden Valley | 40.400 | -105.650 | 2890 | NRCS-SC | 1/1/1941 | Present | Yes |
| Lake Irene | 40.417 | -105.817 | 3261 | NRCS-SC | 1/1/1938 | Present | Yes |
| Longs Peak | 40.267 | -105.583 | 3200 | NRCS-SC | 1/1/1951 | Present | Yes |
| Milner Pass | 40.400 | -105.833 | 2972 | NRCS-SC | 1/1/1952 | Present | Yes |
| North Inlet Grand Lake | 40.283 | -105.767 | 2743 | NRCS-SC | 1/1/1938 | Present | Yes |
| Wild Basin | 40.200 | -105.600 | 2926 | NRCS-SC | 1/1/1936 | Present | Yes |
| Harbison Meadow | 40.271 | -105.833 | 2621 | RAWS | 2/1/2003 | Present | Yes |
| Bear Lake | 40.317 | -105.650 | 2896 | SNOTEL | 10/1/1980 | Present | Yes |
| Copeland Lake | 40.200 | -105.567 | 2621 | SNOTEL | 10/1/1980 | Present | Yes |
| Lake Irene | 40.417 | -105.817 | 3261 | SNOTEL | 10/1/1978 | Present | Yes |
| Phantom Valley | 40.400 | -105.850 | 2752 | SNOTEL | 10/1/1980 | Present | Yes |
| Willow Park | 40.433 | -105.733 | 3261 | SNOTEL | 7/6/1980 | Present | Yes |
| CSU Campus | 40.576 | -105.086 | 1525 | BWFO | M | Present | No |
| CSU Foothills Campus | 40.600 | -105.140 | 1570 | BWFO | M | Present | No |
| NCAR Foothills Lab | 40.035 | -105.243 | 1625 | BWFO | M | Present | No |
| NCAR Table Mesa | 39.978 | -105.276 | 1885 | BWFO | M | Present | No |
| Niwot Ridge Albion | 40.043 | -105.592 | 3259 | BWFO | M | Present | No |
| Niwot Ridge Arickaree Glacier | 40.049 | -105.640 | 3814 | BWFO | M | Present | No |
| Niwot Ridge C1 | 40.036 | -105.544 | 3022 | BWFO | M | Present | No |
| Niwot Ridge D1 | 40.070 | -105.620 | 3743 | BWFO | M | Present | No |
| Niwot Ridge Green Lake 4 | 40.055 | -105.618 | 3571 | BWFO | M | Present | No |
| Niwot Ridge Saddle | 40.056 | -105.589 | 3525 | BWFO | M | Present | No |
| Rocky Flats Nat Wind Tech Ctr | 39.914 | -105.247 | 1855 | BWFO | M | Present | No |
| Rocky Mountain NP | 40.278 | -105.545 | 2743 | CASTNet | 4/1/1987 | Present | No |
| Boulder SH-36 @ Baseline (39) | 39.988 | -105.250 | 1640 | CDOT | M | Present | No |
| Lily Lake (35) | 40.300 | -105.550 | 2743 | CDOT | M | Present | No |
| NOAA (39) | 39.995 | -105.270 | 1678 | CDOT | M | Present | No |
| Taft Ave Loveland (38) | 40.375 | -105.098 | 1536 | CDOT | M | Present | No |
| US 287 @ Fort Collins (38) | 40.596 | -105.072 | 1513 | CDOT | M | Present | No |
| Ward (35) | 40.055 | -105.520 | 3407 | CDOT | M | Present | No |

## Rocky Mountain National Park (ROMO)

| Name | Lat. | Lon. | Elev. (m) | Network | Start | End | In Park? |
|---|---|---|---|---|---|---|---|
| Fort Collins AERC | 40.595 | -105.137 | 1561 | CoAgMet | 2/1/1992 | Present | No |
| Allenspark 2 NNW | 40.188 | -105.502 | 2504 | COOP | 11/1/1944 | Present | No |
| Allenspark 3 NW | 40.229 | -105.518 | 2591 | COOP | 1/1/1994 | 7/1/2004 | No |
| Apex 1 W | 39.867 | -105.583 | 3172 | COOP | 8/1/1966 | 7/31/1976 | No |
| Arapaho Ridge | 40.350 | -106.383 | 3346 | COOP | 1/1/1966 | 12/31/1976 | No |
| Arriba | 40.033 | -105.267 | 1638 | COOP | 1/1/1907 | Present | No |
| Beaver Reservoir | 40.117 | -105.517 | 2794 | COOP | 9/1/1966 | 7/31/1974 | No |
| Beaver Village | 39.917 | -105.783 | 2690 | COOP | M | Present | No |
| Bennett Creek | 40.667 | -105.550 | 2471 | COOP | 9/1/1966 | 7/31/1974 | No |
| Boulder | 40.000 | -105.283 | 1643 | COOP | 10/3/1959 | 5/1/1970 | No |
| Boulder | 39.992 | -105.267 | 1672 | COOP | 10/1/1893 | Present | No |
| Boulder 14 W | 40.035 | -105.541 | 2996 | COOP | 9/29/2003 | Present | No |
| Boulder 2 | 40.034 | -105.281 | 1650 | COOP | 8/1/1948 | Present | No |
| Boulder KBOL | 40.017 | -105.267 | 1671 | COOP | M | Present | No |
| Buckhorn Mtn. 1 E | 40.616 | -105.297 | 2256 | COOP | 6/22/1988 | Present | No |
| Cameron Pass | 40.517 | -105.900 | 3142 | COOP | 1/1/1966 | 12/31/1976 | No |
| Caribou Ranch | 40.000 | -105.517 | 2550 | COOP | 12/1/1962 | 4/13/1970 | No |
| Coal Creek Canyon | 39.896 | -105.385 | 2728 | COOP | 12/9/1993 | Present | No |
| Colorado State Forest | 40.500 | -105.967 | 2827 | COOP | 1/1/1966 | 4/7/1975 | No |
| Deadman Hill | 40.800 | -105.767 | 3123 | COOP | 8/1/1948 | 7/31/1976 | No |
| Drake | 40.433 | -105.339 | 1881 | COOP | 10/1/1974 | Present | No |
| East Portal | 39.900 | -105.633 | 2809 | COOP | 5/1/1968 | 4/30/1975 | No |
| East Ute Pass | 40.817 | -106.050 | 3013 | COOP | 1/1/1966 | 12/31/1976 | No |
| Estes Park | 40.377 | -105.486 | 2280 | COOP | 2/1/1896 | 7/31/2000 | No |
| Estes Park 1 SSE | 40.369 | -105.511 | 2373 | COOP | 7/30/2001 | Present | No |
| Flatiron | 40.369 | -105.235 | 1678 | COOP | 8/29/1996 | Present | No |
| Fort Collins 9 NW | 40.665 | -105.223 | 1591 | COOP | 10/1/1974 | Present | No |
| Fort Collins KCOL | 40.583 | -105.100 | 1534 | COOP | 10/1/1955 | 1/31/1974 | No |
| Fraser | 39.943 | -105.817 | 2609 | COOP | 2/1/1987 | Present | No |
| Fraser | 39.927 | -105.808 | 2681 | COOP | 6/29/2003 | Present | No |
| Glen Comfort | 40.390 | -105.450 | 2240 | COOP | 3/10/1995 | 3/17/1999 | No |
| Glendevey | 40.800 | -105.883 | 2522 | COOP | 8/1/1917 | 6/30/1958 | No |
| Gould 4 SE S F S P | 40.509 | -106.006 | 2743 | COOP | 9/21/1999 | Present | No |
| Granby 8 S | 40.000 | -105.917 | 2652 | COOP | 1/1/1975 | 8/31/1975 | No |
| Grand Lake | 40.233 | -105.850 | 2544 | COOP | 7/1/1952 | 11/30/1958 | No |
| Grand Lake 6 SSW | 40.185 | -105.867 | 2526 | COOP | 8/1/1948 | Present | No |
| Gross Reservoir | 39.936 | -105.350 | 2429 | COOP | 8/1/1968 | Present | No |
| Hawthorne | 39.933 | -105.283 | 1806 | COOP | 8/15/1908 | 6/8/1978 | No |
| Hot Sulphur Springs | 40.050 | -106.133 | 2318 | COOP | 12/1/1941 | 9/30/1981 | No |
| Hourglass Reservoir | 40.583 | -105.632 | 2902 | COOP | 9/1/1988 | Present | No |
| Longmont 2 ESE | 40.159 | -105.074 | 1509 | COOP | 1/1/1893 | 1/1/2005 | No |
| Longmont 6 NW | 40.247 | -105.146 | 1570 | COOP | 8/1/1948 | Present | No |

## Rocky Mountain National Park (ROMO)

| Name | Lat. | Lon. | Elev. (m) | Network | Start | End | In Park? |
|------|------|------|-----------|---------|-------|-----|----------|
| Longs Peak | 40.283 | -105.550 | 2733 | COOP | 8/1/1948 | 7/31/1976 | No |
| Loveland 2 N | 40.435 | -105.085 | 1548 | COOP | 7/1/1989 | Present | No |
| Nederland | 40.036 | -105.546 | 3051 | COOP | 9/9/1996 | Present | No |
| Nederland 2 NNE | 39.983 | -105.500 | 2512 | COOP | 4/1/1970 | 4/1/1989 | No |
| Orodell 1 SW | 40.000 | -105.333 | 1777 | COOP | 6/1/1976 | 3/5/1999 | No |
| Parshall 10 SSE | 39.917 | -106.117 | 2522 | COOP | 5/1/1951 | 4/7/1975 | No |
| Rand | 40.449 | -106.184 | 2630 | COOP | 11/1/1988 | 6/1/1998 | No |
| Red Feather Lakes | 40.798 | -105.586 | 2530 | COOP | 7/1/1991 | 5/27/1997 | No |
| Red Feather Lakes 6 | 40.733 | -105.517 | 2318 | COOP | 10/1/1959 | 8/31/1962 | No |
| Red Feather Lks 2 SE | 40.783 | -105.550 | 2489 | COOP | 9/1/1941 | 7/1/1990 | No |
| Rollinsville | 39.917 | -105.500 | 2586 | COOP | 10/1/1974 | 5/1/1985 | No |
| Rollinsville 1 SE | 39.900 | -105.483 | 2751 | COOP | M | Present | No |
| Rustic 12 WSW | 40.700 | -105.800 | 2463 | COOP | 10/1/1974 | 7/1/1991 | No |
| Rustic 9 WSW | 40.702 | -105.711 | 2347 | COOP | 7/1/1991 | Present | No |
| Silver Lake | 40.033 | -105.576 | 3158 | COOP | 6/13/1910 | 7/24/1996 | No |
| Sky Ranch Lutheran Camp | 40.583 | -105.600 | 2773 | COOP | 6/14/1985 | 8/23/1988 | No |
| Tabernash | 40.000 | -105.850 | 2541 | COOP | 10/1/1950 | 11/30/1951 | No |
| Waterdale | 40.426 | -105.210 | 1594 | COOP | 1/1/1902 | Present | No |
| Williams Fork Dam | 40.038 | -106.204 | 2322 | COOP | 9/1/1963 | Present | No |
| Winter Park | 39.890 | -105.762 | 2775 | COOP | 3/1/1942 | Present | No |
| Allenspark Lodge | 40.200 | -105.533 | 2536 | CRBFC | M | Present | No |
| Winter Park | 39.889 | -105.760 | 2761 | CRBFC | M | Present | No |
| AB0MH-1 Boulder | 40.018 | -105.348 | 2012 | CWOP | M | Present | No |
| AB0MY-2 Boulder | 40.043 | -105.278 | 1590 | CWOP | M | Present | No |
| CW0078 Estes Park | 40.363 | -105.507 | 2380 | CWOP | M | Present | No |
| CW0346 Ft. Collins | 40.496 | -105.055 | 1530 | CWOP | M | Present | No |
| CW0549 Lafayette | 40.003 | -105.141 | 1646 | CWOP | M | Present | No |
| CW1650 Berthoud | 40.323 | -105.182 | 1683 | CWOP | M | Present | No |
| CW1778 Ft. Collins | 40.563 | -105.058 | 1555 | CWOP | M | Present | No |
| CW2056 Ft. Collins | 40.526 | -105.129 | 1609 | CWOP | M | Present | No |
| CW2749 Loveland | 40.454 | -105.067 | 1530 | CWOP | M | Present | No |
| CW2996 Longmont | 40.180 | -105.090 | 1506 | CWOP | M | Present | No |
| CW3065 Estes Park | 40.383 | -105.483 | 2347 | CWOP | M | Present | No |
| CW4671 Loveland | 40.351 | -105.171 | 1622 | CWOP | M | Present | No |
| CW4899 Boulder | 40.046 | -105.246 | 1618 | CWOP | M | Present | No |
| CW5038 Ward | 40.081 | -105.493 | 2850 | CWOP | M | Present | No |
| CW5066 Gilpin Co. | 39.824 | -105.480 | 2856 | CWOP | M | Present | No |
| CW5206 Boulder | 40.138 | -105.238 | 1674 | CWOP | M | Present | No |
| CW5258 Estes Park | 40.383 | -105.507 | 2310 | CWOP | M | Present | No |
| CW5469 Tabernash | 40.007 | -105.886 | 2684 | CWOP | M | Present | No |
| CW5610 Fort Collins | 40.517 | -105.167 | 1776 | CWOP | M | Present | No |
| CW5678 Loveland | 40.443 | -105.025 | 1511 | CWOP | M | Present | No |

## Rocky Mountain National Park (ROMO)

| Name | Lat. | Lon. | Elev. (m) | Network | Start | End | In Park? |
|------|------|------|-----------|---------|-------|-----|----------|
| K0FCC Longmont | 40.194 | -105.067 | 1537 | CWOP | M | Present | No |
| KB0TVJ-5 Boulder | 40.054 | -105.208 | 1582 | CWOP | M | Present | No |
| KB0URX-3 Loveland | 40.432 | -105.086 | 1543 | CWOP | M | Present | No |
| KG0HM-2 Crystal Lakes | 40.859 | -105.637 | 2634 | CWOP | M | Present | No |
| KI0IO-2 Berthoud | 40.300 | -105.082 | 1531 | CWOP | M | Present | No |
| KM6GE Allenspark | 40.180 | -105.478 | 2512 | CWOP | M | Present | No |
| W0RMT Louisville | 39.985 | -105.155 | 1689 | CWOP | M | Present | No |
| WA0BAG-5 Bagg Mtn. | 40.533 | -105.250 | 2177 | CWOP | M | Present | No |
| WM0F Berthoud | 40.345 | -105.100 | 1573 | CWOP | M | Present | No |
| Blue_Mountain | 39.870 | -105.297 | 2454 | DUDFCD | M | Present | No |
| Button_Rock | 40.221 | -105.369 | 1981 | DUDFCD | M | Present | No |
| Cal-Wood_Ranch | 40.148 | -105.390 | 2365 | DUDFCD | M | Present | No |
| Louisville_Lake | 39.992 | -105.153 | 1701 | DUDFCD | M | Present | No |
| Sugarloaf | 40.018 | -105.404 | 2396 | DUDFCD | M | Present | No |
| Ward_C-1 | 40.035 | -105.543 | 2957 | DUDFCD | M | Present | No |
| Salvation Army Camp | 40.278 | -105.545 | 2743 | GPMP | 4/1/1987 | 7/31/1995 | No |
| Boulder | 39.990 | -105.260 | 1670 | GPS-MET | M | Present | No |
| Boulder (FH Lab) | 40.040 | -105.240 | 1625 | GPS-MET | M | Present | No |
| Boulder (Mesa Lab) | 39.980 | -105.270 | 1883 | GPS-MET | M | Present | No |
| Fort Collins | 40.590 | -105.150 | 1611 | GPS-MET | M | Present | No |
| Nederland (Niwot Ridge) | 40.050 | -105.590 | 3526 | GPS-MET | M | Present | No |
| A-1 | 40.010 | -105.376 | 2199 | LTER | M | Present | No |
| Albion Townsite | 40.043 | -105.592 | 3259 | LTER | M | Present | No |
| Arikaree Glacier | 40.055 | -105.619 | 3814 | LTER | M | Present | No |
| B-1 | 40.022 | -105.429 | 2621 | LTER | M | Present | No |
| C-1 | 40.036 | -105.536 | 3021 | LTER | M | Present | No |
| D-1 | 40.059 | -105.617 | 3739 | LTER | M | Present | No |
| Green Lake 4 | 40.049 | -105.640 | 3570 | LTER | M | Present | No |
| Saddle | 40.048 | -105.571 | 3528 | LTER | M | Present | No |
| Soddie | 40.547 | -105.589 | 3345 | LTER | M | Present | No |
| Subnivean | 40.054 | -105.591 | 3535 | LTER | M | Present | No |
| Niwot Ridge-Southeast | 40.036 | -105.536 | 3022 | NADP | 1/24/2006 | Present | No |
| Niwot Saddle | 40.055 | -105.588 | 3520 | NADP | 6/5/1984 | Present | No |
| Sugarloaf | 39.994 | -105.480 | 2524 | NADP | 11/4/1986 | Present | No |
| Baltimore | 39.900 | -105.583 | 2682 | NRCS-SC | 1/1/1961 | Present | No |
| Bennett Creek | 40.667 | -105.617 | 2804 | NRCS-SC | 1/1/1966 | Present | No |
| Berthoud Pass | 39.833 | -105.750 | 2957 | NRCS-SC | 1/1/1936 | Present | No |
| Big South | 40.617 | -105.817 | 2621 | NRCS-SC | 1/1/1936 | Present | No |
| Boulder Falls | 40.017 | -105.567 | 3048 | NRCS-SC | 1/1/1952 | Present | No |
| Cameron Pass | 40.517 | -105.567 | 3135 | NRCS-SC | 1/1/1936 | Present | No |
| Chambers Lake | 40.617 | -105.833 | 2743 | NRCS-SC | 1/1/1936 | Present | No |
| Corral Creek | 40.150 | -106.150 | 2957 | NRCS-SC | 1/1/1995 | Present | No |

## Rocky Mountain National Park (ROMO)

| Name | Lat. | Lon. | Elev. (m) | Network | Start | End | In Park? |
|---|---|---|---|---|---|---|---|
| Deadman Hill | 40.800 | -105.767 | 3115 | NRCS-SC | 1/1/1937 | Present | No |
| Granby | 40.150 | -106.000 | 2621 | NRCS-SC | 1/1/1949 | Present | No |
| Hourglass Lake | 40.583 | -105.633 | 2853 | NRCS-SC | 1/1/1938 | Present | No |
| Lapland | 39.883 | -105.883 | 2835 | NRCS-SC | 1/1/1938 | Present | No |
| Mc Intyre | 40.783 | -105.933 | 2774 | NRCS-SC | 1/1/1949 | Present | No |
| Park View | 40.367 | -106.100 | 2792 | NRCS-SC | 1/1/1936 | Present | No |
| Ranch Creek | 39.933 | -105.733 | 2865 | NRCS-SC | 1/1/1957 | Present | No |
| Red Feather | 40.817 | -105.650 | 2743 | NRCS-SC | 1/1/1991 | Present | No |
| Sawtooth | 40.133 | -105.583 | 2969 | NRCS-SC | 1/1/2002 | Present | No |
| University Camp | 40.033 | -105.567 | 3139 | NRCS-SC | 1/1/1938 | Present | No |
| Vasquez | 39.850 | -105.817 | 2926 | NRCS-SC | 1/1/1957 | Present | No |
| Ward | 40.067 | -105.517 | 2896 | NRCS-SC | 1/1/1950 | Present | No |
| Willow Creek Pass | 40.350 | -106.100 | 2908 | NRCS-SC | 1/1/1938 | Present | No |
| Salvation Army Camp portable | 40.278 | -105.545 | 2743 | POMS | 7/1/2002 | Present | No |
| Estes Park | 40.367 | -105.550 | 2384 | RAWS | 3/1/2001 | Present | No |
| Gunsight | 40.209 | -106.329 | 2566 | RAWS | 10/1/1987 | Present | No |
| Pickle Gulch | 39.874 | -105.516 | 2859 | RAWS | 5/1/2000 | Present | No |
| Red Feather | 40.798 | -105.572 | 2499 | RAWS | 5/1/1985 | Present | No |
| Redstone | 40.571 | -105.226 | 1854 | RAWS | 2/1/2003 | Present | No |
| Sugarloaf | 40.018 | -105.361 | 2052 | RAWS | 5/1/2001 | Present | No |
| Fort Collins | 40.615 | -105.131 | 1525 | SAO | 1/1/1893 | Present | No |
| Fraser | 39.950 | -105.833 | 2610 | SAO | 6/20/1908 | 10/25/1974 | No |
| Winter Park | 39.883 | -105.767 | 2770 | SAO | 8/1/1985 | Present | No |
| Arrow | 39.917 | -105.750 | 2950 | SNOTEL | 10/1/1978 | Present | No |
| Deadman Hill | 40.800 | -105.767 | 3115 | SNOTEL | 10/1/1978 | Present | No |
| Joe Wright | 40.533 | -105.883 | 3085 | SNOTEL | 10/1/1978 | Present | No |
| Lake Eldora | 39.933 | -105.583 | 2957 | SNOTEL | 10/1/1978 | Present | No |
| Niwot | 40.033 | -105.550 | 3021 | SNOTEL | 10/1/1980 | Present | No |
| Stillwater Creek | 40.233 | -105.917 | 2658 | SNOTEL | 11/1/1985 | Present | No |
| University Camp | 40.033 | -105.567 | 3139 | SNOTEL | 10/1/1978 | Present | No |
| Willow Creek Pass | 40.350 | -106.100 | 2908 | SNOTEL | 10/1/1978 | Present | No |
| Boulder Erl | 40.017 | -105.283 | 1701 | WBAN | 1/1/1979 | 3/31/1980 | No |
| East Portal | 39.900 | -105.650 | 2805 | WBAN | 9/1/1945 | 4/30/1946 | No |
| Niwot Ridge | 40.050 | -105.583 | 3475 | WBAN | 5/11/1983 | Present | No |
| Table Mountain | 40.133 | -105.233 | 1689 | WBAN | 3/1/1995 | Present | No |
| Boulder | 40.090 | -105.340 | 2038 | WX4U | M | Present | No |

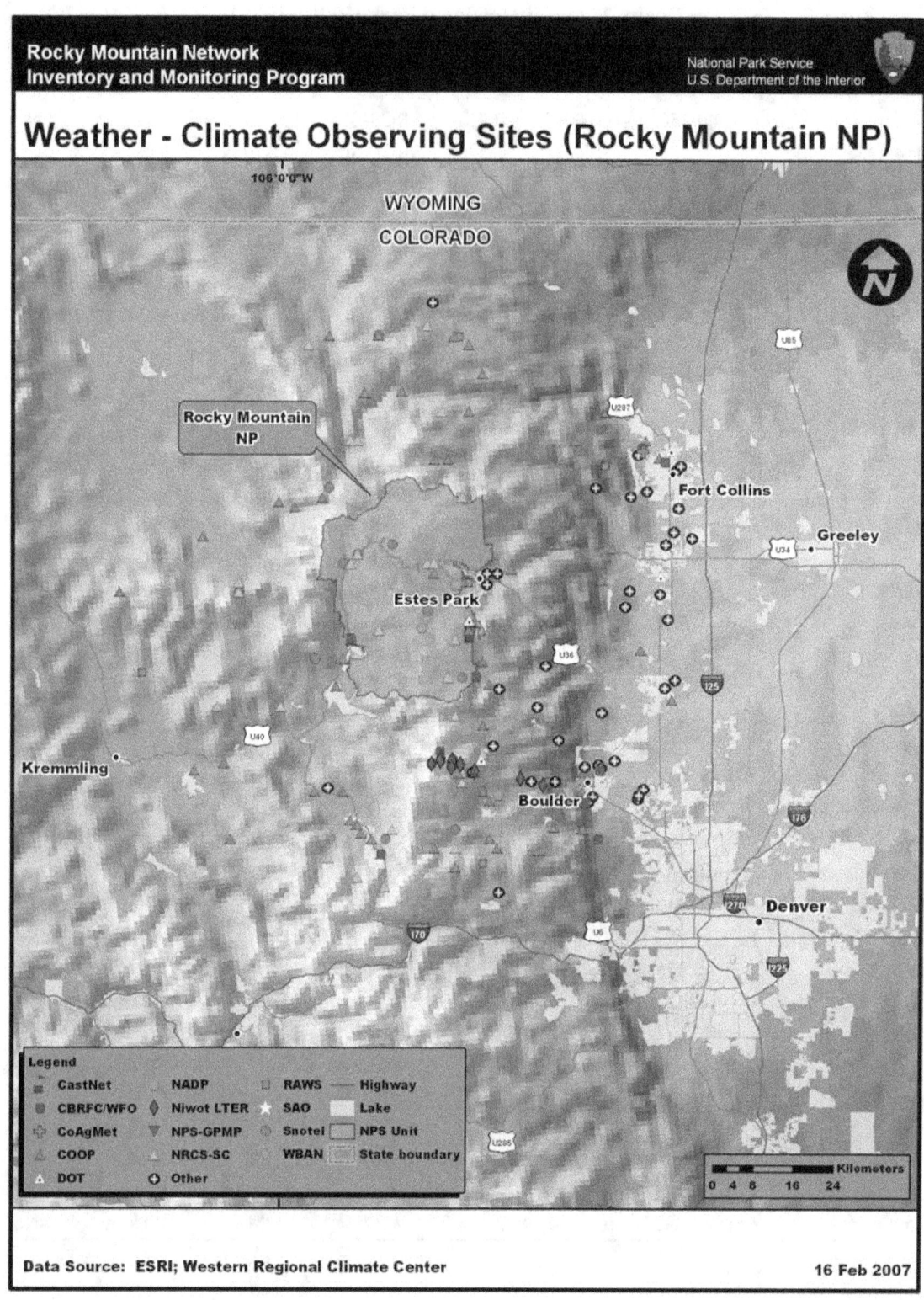

Figure 4.3. Station locations for Rocky Mountain National Park.

since 1902. Its data record is largely complete, with scattered, small data gaps throughout. The COOP station "Arriba" (1907-present) is 29 km southeast of ROMO. Its data record is unreliable. The COOP station "Estes Park" started in 1896 and provided a long-term data record near the east entrance of ROMO, but this station unfortunately quit taking observations in 2000.

A few other active COOP climate stations around ROMO have data records extending back to the 1940s and 1950s. Other manual sites within 40 km of the boundaries of GRSA include three NADP stations south and east of ROMO, including sites along Niwot Ridge, south of ROMO (Figure 4.3), and numerous NRCS-SC sites. Niwot Ridge also includes an array of 10 automated weather stations with the U.S. Long Term Ecological Research Network (LTER). These are high quality weather stations providing valuable near-real-time weather information for the alpine environments south of ROMO.

A suite of air-quality monitoring stations that also measure meteorological elements is located just outside ROMO near Goblins Castle Road, just a few kilometers north of the Longs Peak entrance in southeastern ROMO (Figure 4.3). These stations include a CASTNet site (Rocky Mountain NP), a GPMP site (Salvation Army Camp), and a POMS site (Salvation Army Camp portable),

Six stations were identified with the DUDFCD network (Table 4.5). These are automated stations that are mostly southeast of ROMO. Five stations were identified with the GPS-MET network. These stations are located primarily along the Front Range, south and east of ROMO.

The six RAWS stations we identified within 40 km of ROMO are all active and have very reliable data records. The closest weather station, "Estes Park" (2001-present) is just east of ROMO (Figure 4.3). The longest records come from the RAWS stations "Red Feather" (1985-present), 29 km north of ROMO, and "Gunsight" (1987-present), 40 km west of ROMO.

Three SAO stations, two active, were identified within 40 km of ROMO. "Fort Collins" (34 km northeast of ROMO) has the longest data record, with over 100 years of data (1893-present). The other active SAO station, "Winter Park" (1985-present), is 31 km south of ROMO.

Eight SNOTEL stations were identified within 40 km of ROMO (Table 4.5). The closest stations ("Joe Wright" and "Stillwater Creek") are a few kilometers north and west of ROMO. With the exception of "Deadman Hill" (28 km north of ROMO), the remaining SNOTEL stations are generally in the mountains south of the park unit.

### 4.2.5. Florissant Fossil Beds National Monument
One station was identified within the boundaries of FLFO (Table 4.6; Figure 4.4). This is a COOP station, "Florissant Fossil Beds." While the data record indicates that the climate station has been active since 1948, there are no data available until December 1989.

Out of the 21 COOP stations identified within 40 km of the boundaries of FLFO, eight are active (Table 4.6). The longest record we identified among these active stations was from the COOP station "Cheesman," 31 km north of FLFO. This station has been active since 1902 and its data record is very complete. The COOP station "Lake George 8 SW" is 14 km west of FLFO and

Table 4.6. Weather and climate stations for the ROMN park units in southern Colorado. Stations inside park units and within 40 km of the park unit boundary are included. Missing entries are indicated by "M".

| Name | Lat. | Lon. | Elev. (m) | Network | Start | End | In Park? |
|---|---|---|---|---|---|---|---|
| **Florissant Fossil Beds National Monument (FLFO)** | | | | | | | |
| Florissant Fossil Beds | 38.913 | -105.285 | 2554 | COOP | 8/1/1948 | Present | Yes |
| South Park Mountain (NREL) | 39.270 | -105.620 | 2944 | BWFO | M | Present | No |
| 21st Street (85) | 38.840 | -104.859 | 1881 | CDOT | M | Present | No |
| Centennial & Allegheny S.(85) | 38.930 | -104.865 | 2067 | CDOT | M | Present | No |
| Garden of the Gods (85) | 38.895 | -104.830 | 1932 | CDOT | M | Present | No |
| I-24 at Fountain Creek (85) | 38.860 | -104.873 | 1935 | CDOT | M | Present | No |
| I-25 @ Fountain Creek (85*) | 38.860 | -104.870 | 1887 | CDOT | M | Present | No |
| Jamboree & Chapel Hills (85) | 38.952 | -104.792 | 2006 | CDOT | M | Present | No |
| Monument Hill (84) | 39.100 | -104.855 | 2207 | CDOT | M | Present | No |
| Monument Hill (85*) | 39.100 | -104.855 | 2168 | CDOT | M | Present | No |
| Pikes Peak & Union (85) | 38.833 | -104.795 | 1870 | CDOT | M | Present | No |
| Star Ranch & Hwy 115 (85) | 38.775 | -104.815 | 1843 | CDOT | M | Present | No |
| Wilkerson Pass (37) | 39.045 | -105.574 | 2865 | CDOT | M | Present | No |
| Cheesman | 39.220 | -105.278 | 2097 | COOP | 8/1/1902 | Present | No |
| Colorado Springs 3 N | 38.850 | -104.833 | 1861 | COOP | 1/1/1931 | 6/30/1948 | No |
| Cripple Creek | 38.750 | -105.180 | 2911 | COOP | 9/1/1896 | 2/25/2003 | No |
| Cripple Creek 3 NNW | 38.796 | -105.200 | 2815 | COOP | 9/1/2005 | Present | No |
| Deckers | 39.250 | -105.233 | 1981 | COOP | 5/1/1981 | 8/1/1991 | No |
| Fremont Experimental | 38.850 | -104.950 | 2699 | COOP | 1/1/1931 | 12/31/1936 | No |
| Guffey | 38.750 | -105.533 | 2623 | COOP | 8/1/1948 | 7/31/1950 | No |
| Guffey 10 SE | 38.675 | -105.392 | 2620 | COOP | 6/1/1950 | Present | No |
| Guffey 5 N | 38.817 | -105.533 | 2745 | COOP | 5/31/1940 | 11/30/1951 | No |
| Lake George 8 SW | 38.908 | -105.471 | 2606 | COOP | 8/1/1948 | Present | No |
| Lake Moraine | 38.817 | -104.983 | 3128 | COOP | 5/11/1894 | 9/24/1991 | No |
| Manitou Springs | 38.856 | -104.933 | 2021 | COOP | 8/1/1948 | Present | No |
| Manitou Springs City | 38.867 | -104.917 | 1955 | COOP | 1/1/1961 | 1/31/1971 | No |
| Monument | 39.103 | -104.868 | 2158 | COOP | 6/7/1988 | 6/1/2003 | No |
| Monument 1 SSE | 39.081 | -104.866 | 2114 | COOP | 1/16/2004 | Present | No |
| Monument 2 WSW | 39.083 | -104.917 | 2239 | COOP | 1/1/1911 | 7/12/1965 | No |
| Palmer Lake | 39.117 | -104.917 | 2201 | COOP | 8/1/1899 | 3/31/1986 | No |
| Ruxton Park | 38.842 | -104.974 | 2758 | COOP | 9/1/1959 | Present | No |
| Victor | 38.717 | -105.150 | 2959 | COOP | 2/17/1904 | 6/8/1978 | No |
| Westcreek | 39.133 | -105.117 | 2379 | COOP | 8/1/1948 | 9/30/1959 | No |
| Woodland Park 8 NNW | 39.101 | -105.094 | 2365 | COOP | 8/1/1948 | Present | No |
| CW1080 Colorado Springs | 38.797 | -104.852 | 1865 | CWOP | M | Present | No |
| CW1505 Florissant | 38.954 | -105.267 | 2673 | CWOP | M | Present | No |
| CW2088 Monument | 39.058 | -104.831 | 2137 | CWOP | M | Present | No |
| CW2417 Westcreek | 39.239 | -105.273 | 2384 | CWOP | M | Present | No |
| CW2423 Trumbull | 39.264 | -105.220 | 1981 | CWOP | M | Present | No |

| Name | Lat. | Lon. | Elev. (m) | Network | Start | End | In Park? |
|---|---|---|---|---|---|---|---|
| CW2960 Guffey | 38.757 | -105.473 | 2806 | CWOP | M | Present | No |
| CW4498 Colorado Springs | 38.922 | -104.880 | 2149 | CWOP | M | Present | No |
| CW5115 Florissant | 38.981 | -105.244 | 2713 | CWOP | M | Present | No |
| CW5171 Colorado Springs | 38.928 | -104.868 | 2027 | CWOP | M | Present | No |
| CW5248 Woodland Park | 39.049 | -105.057 | 2543 | CWOP | M | Present | No |
| CW5608 Colorado Springs | 38.944 | -104.871 | 2075 | CWOP | M | Present | No |
| K0RM Colorado Springs | 38.928 | -104.830 | 2014 | CWOP | M | Present | No |
| KA0MWA-1 Westcreek | 39.239 | -105.273 | 2384 | CWOP | M | Present | No |
| KC0LNO-1 Monument | 39.084 | -104.872 | 2109 | CWOP | M | Present | No |
| W0DVM Divide | 38.901 | -105.208 | 2873 | CWOP | M | Present | No |
| WA6GZC-1 Colorado Springs | 38.811 | -104.850 | 1831 | CWOP | M | Present | No |
| WE1A USAF Academy | 38.990 | -104.874 | 2094 | CWOP | M | Present | No |
| Manitou | 39.101 | -105.093 | 2362 | NADP | 10/17/1978 | Present | No |
| Eleven Mile | 38.950 | -105.533 | 2618 | NRCS-SC | 1/1/1983 | Present | No |
| 9J Road | 39.159 | -105.224 | 2538 | RAWS | 8/1/2002 | 6/30/2005 | No |
| Cheeseman | 39.181 | -105.267 | 2286 | RAWS | 2/1/1987 | Present | No |
| Hackett | 39.074 | -105.295 | 2822 | RAWS | 8/1/2002 | Present | No |
| Lake George | 38.977 | -105.355 | 2281 | RAWS | 5/1/1991 | Present | No |
| Manchester | 39.105 | -105.138 | 2587 | RAWS | 12/1/2004 | Present | No |
| Matacat | 39.093 | -105.376 | 2685 | RAWS | 7/1/2002 | Present | No |
| Polhemus | 39.255 | -105.132 | 2647 | RAWS | 12/1/2004 | Present | No |
| PSF4 | 38.978 | -105.355 | 2469 | RAWS | 7/1/2002 | 7/31/2003 | No |
| Thompson Mtn. | 38.620 | -105.391 | 2580 | RAWS | 2/1/2003 | Present | No |
| USAF Academy | 38.967 | -104.817 | 2003 | SAO | 11/1/1967 | Present | No |
| Divide | 38.933 | -105.150 | 2774 | WBAN | 4/1/1946 | 2/28/1949 | No |

| Grand Sand Dunes National Park and Preserve (GRSA) | | | | | | | |
|---|---|---|---|---|---|---|---|
| Great Sand Dunes | 37.733 | -105.512 | 2494 | COOP | 9/1/1950 | Present | Yes |
| Great Sand Dunes HQ | 37.725 | -105.517 | 2487 | GPMP | 3/1/1988 | 9/30/1991 | Yes |
| Great Sand Dunes | 37.727 | -105.511 | 2537 | RAWS | 1/1/2004 | Present | Yes |
| Medano Pass | 37.833 | -105.433 | 2932 | SNOTEL | M | Present | Yes |
| La Veta Pass (74) | 37.610 | -105.200 | 2834 | CDOT | M | Present | No |
| Blanca | 37.391 | -105.557 | 2364 | CoAgMet | 2/24/1997 | Present | No |
| Center | 37.707 | -106.144 | 2348 | CoAgMet | 10/8/1993 | Present | No |
| Center #2 | 37.829 | -106.038 | 2319 | CoAgMet | 10/2/2003 | Present | No |
| Alamosa | 37.467 | -105.883 | 2297 | COOP | 5/1/1906 | 12/31/1949 | No |
| Alamosa 1 NW | 37.483 | -105.883 | 2295 | COOP | 8/1/1948 | 10/15/1999 | No |
| Alamosa 2 S | 37.442 | -105.861 | 2296 | COOP | 7/1/2005 | Present | No |
| Center 4 SSW | 37.707 | -106.144 | 2339 | COOP | 8/1/1941 | Present | No |
| Crestone 1 SE | 37.987 | -105.687 | 2473 | COOP | 3/15/1982 | Present | No |
| Fort Garland | 37.433 | -105.433 | M | COOP | M | Present | No |
| Froze Creek | 38.000 | -105.333 | 2501 | COOP | 8/1/1948 | 12/31/1949 | No |
| Gardner | 37.767 | -105.183 | 2123 | COOP | 6/1/1939 | 7/23/1971 | No |
| Garnett | 37.717 | -106.000 | 2312 | COOP | 1/1/1931 | 12/31/1941 | No |
| La Veta Pass | 37.467 | -105.167 | 2818 | COOP | 3/1/1909 | 1/31/1954 | No |
| Monte Vista 2 N | 37.617 | -106.150 | 2333 | COOP | 8/1/1948 | 1/3/1996 | No |

| Name | Lat. | Lon. | Elev. (m) | Network | Start | End | In Park? |
|---|---|---|---|---|---|---|---|
| Mule Shoe Lodge 1 S | 37.583 | -105.183 | 2704 | COOP | 12/1/1939 | 10/1/1985 | No |
| Red Wing 1 WSW | 37.717 | -105.317 | 2408 | COOP | 4/15/1982 | 2/1/1996 | No |
| San Isabel | 37.983 | -105.050 | 2589 | COOP | 1/1/1938 | 12/31/1943 | No |
| San Luis Lakes 3 W | 37.650 | -105.800 | 2297 | COOP | 5/16/1946 | 7/31/1955 | No |
| Sheep Mountain | 37.715 | -105.235 | 2363 | COOP | 10/1/1987 | Present | No |
| Waverly 1 W | 37.430 | -106.032 | 2317 | COOP | 3/11/2004 | Present | No |
| Westcliffe | 38.131 | -105.466 | 2396 | COOP | 7/1/1895 | Present | No |
| Wetmore 8 SW | 38.133 | -105.200 | 2377 | COOP | 11/1/1949 | 6/30/1953 | No |
| CW4105 Silver Cliff | 38.133 | -105.449 | 2432 | CWOP | M | Present | No |
| Alamosa | 37.441 | -105.865 | 2298 | NADP | 4/22/1980 | Present | No |
| Brown Cabin | 37.550 | -105.400 | 2926 | NRCS-SC | 1/1/1965 | Present | No |
| La Veta Pass | 37.600 | -105.200 | 2877 | NRCS-SC | 1/1/1938 | Present | No |
| Ute Creek | 37.617 | -105.367 | 3246 | NRCS-SC | 1/1/1996 | Present | No |
| Black Mountain | 37.862 | -105.284 | 2738 | RAWS | 7/1/2003 | Present | No |
| Canon City | 38.287 | -105.681 | 2494 | RAWS | 4/1/2001 | Present | No |
| Copper Gulch | 38.314 | -105.484 | 2365 | RAWS | 5/1/1991 | Present | No |
| Sullivan Creek | 38.287 | -105.681 | 2503 | RAWS | 6/1/1996 | 12/31/1999 | No |
| Willis Creek | 38.004 | -105.056 | 2804 | RAWS | 12/1/1989 | Present | No |
| Alamosa | 37.439 | -105.861 | 2296 | SAO | 1/1/1945 | Present | No |
| Blanca | 37.479 | -105.572 | 2350 | SAO | 1/1/1909 | Present | No |
| La Veta Pass | 37.500 | -105.167 | 3114 | SAO | M | Present | No |
| South Colony | 37.967 | -105.533 | 3292 | SNOTEL | 10/1/1991 | Present | No |
| Fort Garland | 37.433 | -105.517 | 2438 | WBAN | 2/1/1938 | 7/31/1938 | No |
| Monte Vista | 37.533 | -106.050 | 2320 | WBAN | 3/1/1939 | 1/31/1960 | No |
| Crestone | 37.580 | -105.410 | 3280 | WX4U | M | Present | No |

except for a data gap through the 1950s, has a reliable data record (1948-present). "Manitou Springs" (28 km east of FLFO) and "Woodland Park 8 NNW" (23 km northeast of FLFO) also have data records going back to 1948. "Guffey 10 SE," 24 km southwest of FLFO, is a precipitation-only COOP station with a very complete record (1950-present). The COOP station "Ruxton" is 25 km southeast of FLFO and has a reliable data record (1959-present).

Several RAWS stations are located within 40 km of FLFO and provide the most reliable source of automated weather data for the park unit (Table 4.6). Most of these are north of FLFO (Figure 4.4). The longest record is at the RAWS station "Cheeseman," 27 km north of FLFO. This station has a very complete record going back to 1987. The closest RAWS station to FLFO is "Lake George," 6 km northwest of FLFO. This station has a very complete record going back to 1991. The other active RAWS stations have data records starting in the early 2000s. In addition to the RAWS stations we identified, the SAO station "USAF Academy" provides near-real-time data 37 km east of FLFO. This SAO station has been active since 1967.

Numerous CDOT and CWOP stations provide automated data within 40 km of FLFO. The CDOT stations are located along major roadways all around FLFO. However, most of the CWOP stations we've identified are east of FLFO, in the Colorado Springs area.

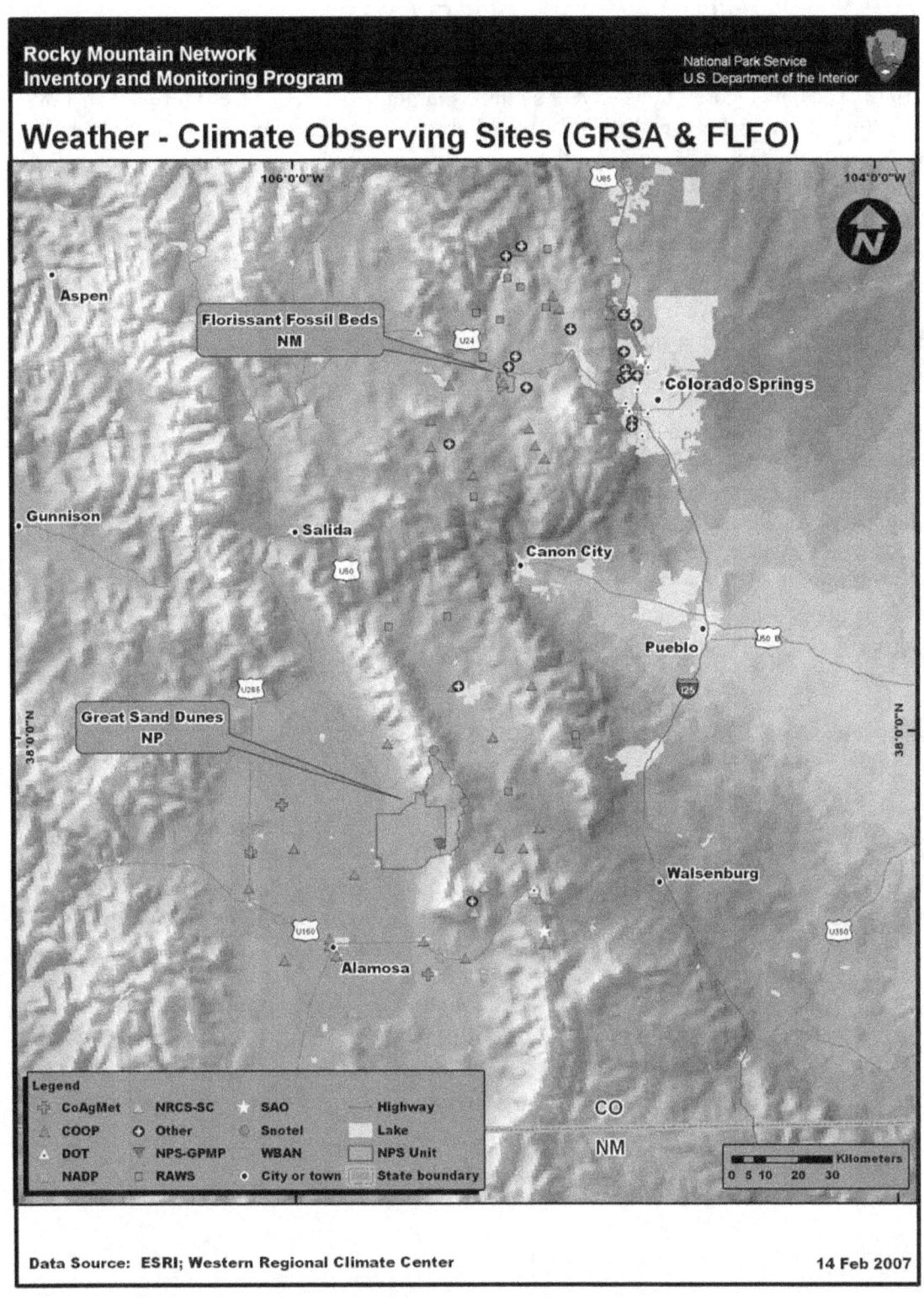

Figure 4.4. Station locations for the ROMN park units in southern Colorado.

### 4.2.6. Great Sand Dunes National Park and Preserve

We identified four stations within the boundaries of GRSA (Table 4.6). The COOP station, "Great Sand Dunes" is an active climate station which has been operating in southern GRSA since 1950. The data record at this COOP station is largely complete except for gaps in 1987 (August, September, and November) and 1988 (February through May). The RAWS weather station "Great Sand Dunes," also in southern GRSA, has provided automated data since 2004. The data record at this RAWS site shows a gap from February to May of 2004. The SNOTEL station "Medano Pass" is currently operating in northeastern GRSA. A GPMP station operated at GRSA headquarters from 1988 to 1991.

Three CoAgMet stations were identified within 40 km of the boundaries of GRSA. These weather stations are all active currently (Table 4.6) and are generally located south and west of GRSA, in the San Luis Valley (Figure 4.4).

Nineteen COOP stations were identified within 40 km of the boundaries of GRSA. Seven of these are active currently (Table 4.6). The longest record we identified among these active climate stations was from the COOP station "Westcliffe," 20 km north of GRSA. This station has been active since 1895 and its data record is largely complete, with scattered data gaps. The last major data gap occurred from June through October of 1995. The COOP station "Center 4 SSW," 37 km west of GRSA, has been active since 1941 and its data record is largely complete, except for a gap in March through August of 1994. Other manual sites within 40 km of the boundaries of GRSA include the NADP station "Alamosa" (1980-present), 28 km southwest of GRSA, and three NRCS-SC sites located in the Sangre de Cristo mountains southeast of GRSA.

Besides the RAWS station within GRSA (Little Bighorn), we have identified four other active RAWS stations that provide near-real-time data within 40 km of the park unit (Table 4.6). The longest record is at the RAWS station "Willis Creek," 37 km northeast of GRSA (Figure 4.4). This station's data record is quite reliable. The RAWS station "Copper Gulch" is 40 km northeast of GRSA and has a reliable data record (1991-present). "Canon City" (2001-present), 39 km northeast of GRSA, has been unreliable since December 2005. The closest RAWS station, however, is "Black Mountain," 13 km northeast of GRSA in the Sangre de Cristo mountain range. This station's data record (2003-present) is quite reliable.

Three SAO stations, all active, are present within 40 km of GRSA. "Blanca" and "Alamosa" are south and west of GRSA and have long data records, while "La Veta Pass" is southeast of GRSA. One SNOTEL station was identified within 40 km of GRSA. "South Colony" is 1 km north of GRSA and has been operating since 1991.

# 5.0. Conclusions and Recommendations

We have based our findings on an examination of available climate records within ROMN units, discussions with NPS staff and other collaborators, and prior knowledge of the area. Here, we offer an evaluation and general comments pertaining to the status, prospects, and needs for climate-monitoring capabilities in ROMN.

## 5.1. Rocky Mountain Inventory and Monitoring Network

Numerous weather and climate networks have stations located within 40 km of ROMN park units. This provides ample opportunities for the ROMN park units to obtain weather and climate data specifically suited for various types of research projects in the park units. Local automated networks are present in and near both GLAC and ROMO that are intended to document the unique conditions experienced in alpine environments. This includes the GNP network in GLAC, concentrated mostly in the Many Glacier area, and the LTER network south of ROMO, on Niwot Ridge.

Long-term climate stations have recently ceased operating near some of the ROMN park units, decreasing the ability of this inventory to identify very long-term climate records that could be used to document climate changes across the ROMN. These losses are particularly noticeable for FLFO, GLAC, and ROMO. In FLFO, the COOP stations "Cripple Creek" (1896-2003) and even "Lake Moraine" (1894-1991) were useful climate records. In GLAC, the COOP station "Kalispell" was a valuable long-term climate record that stopped very recently (1896-2006). In ROMO, Estes Park had a COOP station that ceased taking measurements in 2000. It had been active since 1896. Even when long-term sites have been identified that are still active, there are sometimes questions about whether these records actually come from multiple stations, as may be the case with the COOP stations "Deer Lodge 2" (1893-present) and "Anaconda" (1894-present), identified near GRKO. Caution must be exercised when utilizing such records. Climate monitoring efforts within the ROMN will benefit by encouraging the continued operation of those active climate stations having longer climate records, as these records provide valuable documentation of ongoing climate changes within ROMN park units.

Most of the weather and climate stations we have identified for GLAC are located either at or near the Many Glacier area or they are located around the periphery of the park unit. These peripheral stations are concentrated primarily at West Glacier and along U.S. Highway 2, just south of GLAC. There are notable holes in weather and climate station coverage within GLAC, especially in northwestern GLAC and in southern GLAC. Possible ways to address this coverage gap would be to complement the existing manual stations at St. Marys, at the east entrance to GLAC, with an automated station such as a RAWS site. It may be worth considering expanding the GNP network in the park at locations such as the end of Two Medicine Road in the southeastern portion of the park unit. This would help address the current coverage gaps in southern GLAC. In northwestern GLAC, a GNP station in the vicinity of Bowman Lake would be useful and would be fairly accessible due to maintained roads that are in this area. If funding issues prohibit such installations, the NPS could still consider encouraging local agencies to install RAWS stations (for wildfire research efforts) and/or SNOTEL stations (for snowpack research in GLAC). Both of these networks already have a strong presence in the region.

Few near-real-time weather stations exist currently within the immediate vicinity of GRKO. The only such stations we have identified in this report are MT DOT stations, concentrated along Interstate 90 and U.S. Highway 12, to the north and east of the park unit. Weather and climate monitoring efforts in and around GRKO would likely benefit by having a closer source of near-real-time weather data. There are large portions of the Clark Fork Valley around GRKO that are used agriculturally. With this in mind, it could be beneficial for the NPS to work with NRCS to have a Soil Climate Analysis Network (SCAN) station installed in the area near GRKO. One of the primary goals of the SCAN network is to provide weather conditions in agricultural areas.

Despite the relatively small number of weather and climate stations we identified around LIBI, the park unit does have a source of near-real-time data within the park (RAWS), along with climate stations having data records of several decades in length near the park unit. However, the NPS should encourage the continued operation of those stations having longer climate records near LIBI.

The majority of stations we have identified for ROMO are concentrated at the east and west entrances of the park unit and along Trail Ridge Road (U.S. Highway 34), which runs roughly east-west through the north-central portion of ROMO. The more remote portions of ROMO, i.e., extreme northern ROMO and southwestern ROMO, remain largely unsampled, particularly with regards to near-real-time weather data. In these less-sampled regions, the NPS may want to consider partnering with NRCS to encourage the transition of existing NRCS-SC sites into SNOTEL sites.

For FLFO, station coverage is satisfactory due to the presence of both near-real-time stations and longer-term climate stations in the area. Climate monitoring efforts at FLFO will benefit by maintaining the COOP station that is currently in the park unit ("Florissant Fossil Beds;" 1948-present). If it is desired that near-real-time weather data be measured within FLFO, we would recommend that NPS work with local agencies to install a RAWS station in the park unit. The RAWS network already has considerable station coverage in the area north of FLFO, but this coverage could be expanded southward, as there are currently no RAWS stations in those areas immediately at and to the south of FLFO.

Weather/climate station coverage within GRSA is largely non-existent away from the eastern part of the park unit. Most of the stations we have identified are located near the main visitor center in southeastern GRSA. The NPS may want to consider installing a RAWS station along the jeep road that runs north and east of the visitor center, towards Medano Pass. In southwestern GRSA, suitable sites for near-real-time stations may be found near 6N Lane and Medano Road (10N Lane), in those areas near Head and San Luis Lakes. Even in the higher elevations of eastern GRSA, additional SNOTEL stations may be desirable to better sample the montane and alpine environments of GRSA.

## 5.2. Spatial Variations in Mean Climate

With local variations over short horizontal and vertical distances, topography introduces considerable fine-scale structure to mean climate (temperature and precipitation) within the ROMN park units. Issues encountered in mapping mean climate are discussed in Appendix D and in Redmond et al. (2005).

For areas where new stations will be installed, if only a few new stations will be emplaced, the primary goal should be overall characterization of the main climate elements (temperature and precipitation and their joint relative, snow). This level of characterization generally requires that (a) stations should not be located in deep valley bottoms (cold air drainage pockets) or near excessively steep slopes and (b) stations should be distributed spatially in the major biomes of each park. If such stations already are present in the vicinity, then additional stations would be best used for two important and somewhat competing purposes: (a) add redundancy as backup for loss of data from current stations (or loss of the physical stations) or (b) provide added information on spatial heterogeneity in climate arising from topographic diversity.

## 5.3. Climate Change Detection

There is much interest in the ROMN park units regarding responses to possible future climate changes, such as trends in snowpack and glacier extent (in GLAC and ROMO) and ecosystem adaptations (all park units). In particular, if temperatures continue to warm and montane habitats shrink, as expected, local extinction of some species is likely.

The desire for credible, accurate, complete, and long-term climate records—from any location—cannot be overemphasized. Thus, this consideration always should have a high priority. However, because of spatial diversity in climate, monitoring that fills knowledge gaps and provides information on long-term temporal variability in short-distance relationships also will be valuable. We cannot be sure that climate variability and climate change will affect all parts of a given park unit equally. In fact, it is appropriate to speculate that this is not the case, and spatial variations in temporal variability extend to small spatial scales, a consequence of diversity within ROMN in both topography and in land use patterns.

## 5.4. Aesthetics

This issue arises frequently enough to deserve comment. Standards for quality climate measurements require open exposures away from heat sources, buildings, pavement, close vegetation and tall trees, and human intrusion (thus away from property lines). By their nature, sites that meet these standards are usually quite visible. In many settings (such as heavily forested areas) these sites also are quite rare, making them precisely the same places that managers wish to protect from aesthetic intrusion. The most suitable and scientifically defensible sites frequently are rejected as candidate locations for weather/climate stations. Most weather/climate stations, therefore, tend to be "hidden" but many of these hidden locations have inferior exposures. Some measure of compromise is nearly always called for in siting weather and climate stations.

The public has vast interest and curiosity in weather and climate, and within the NPS I&M networks, such measurements consistently rate near or at the top of desired public information. There seem to be many possible opportunities for exploiting and embracing this widespread interest within the interpretive mission of the NPS. One way to do this would be to highlight rather than hide these stations and educate the public about the need for adequate siting. A number of weather displays we have encountered during visits have proven inadvertently to serve as counterexamples for how measurements should not be made.

## 5.5. Information Access

Access to information promotes its use, which in turn promotes attention to station care and maintenance, better data, and more use. An end-to-end view that extends from sensing to decision support is far preferable to isolated and disconnected activities and aids the support infrastructure that is ultimately so necessary for successful, long-term climate monitoring.

Decisions about improvements in monitoring capacity are facilitated greatly by the ability to examine available climate information. Various methods are being created at WRCC to improve access to that information. Web pages providing historic and ongoing climate data, and information from ROMN park units can be accessed at http://www.wrcc.dri.edu/nps. In the event that this URL changes, there still will be links from the main WRCC Web page entitled "Projects" under NPS.

The WRCC has been steadily developing software to summarize data from hourly sites. This has been occurring under the aegis of the RAWS program and a growing array of product generators ranging from daily and monthly data lists to wind roses and hourly frequency distributions. All park data are available to park personnel via an access code (needed only for data listings) that can be acquired by request. The WRCC RAWS Web page is located at http://www.wrcc.dri.edu/wraws or http://www.raws.dri.edu.

Web pages have been developed to provide access not only to historic and ongoing climate data and information from ROMN park units but also to climate-monitoring efforts for ROMN. These pages can be found through http://www.wrcc.dri.edu/nps.

Additional access to more standard climate information is accessible though the previously mentioned Web pages, as well as through http://www.wrcc.dri.edu/summary. These summaries are generally for COOP stations.

## 5.6. Summarized Conclusions and Recommendations

- Various weather and climate networks identified in and around ROMN park units provide climate data suitable for various types of research projects. Local automated networks such as GNP (GLAC) and LTER (near ROMO) document unique weather and climate conditions experienced in alpine environments.
- The recent loss of active long-term climate records around some ROMN park units (e.g., FLFO, GLAC, and ROMO) negatively affects ability to document climate changes across the ROMN. Some long-term records near GRKO may be composed of records from multiple stations.
- Station coverage in GLAC is primarily at Many Glacier and around periphery of park unit. Coverage gaps exist currently in northwestern and southern GLAC. Suitable sites to address current coverage gaps include Two Medicine Road and Bowman Lake. Suitable networks for new stations include the GNP, RAWS, and SNOTEL networks, depending on the desired use of such data (e.g., monitoring wildfire, snowpack characteristics)
- Near-real-time weather data are not available in immediate vicinity of GRKO. Due to agricultural setting of GRKO, NPS could consider working with NRCS to install a SCAN station in the area.

- FLFO and LIBI appear to have satisfactory station coverage for their purposes, with the presence of both near-real-time weather stations and long-term climate stations in and near the park units. If near-real-time weather data are desired inside FLFO, NPS could consider installing a RAWS station and thus expanding the coverage of the RAWS network southward into the FLFO region.
- Weather and climate station coverage within GRSA is primarily in far eastern GRSA, especially near main visitor center. NPS may consider new RAWS installations in southwestern GRSA station (e.g., near 6N Lane and/or Medano Road) and along the jeep road that runs north and east of the visitor center, towards Medano Pass. Additional SNOTEL stations at the higher elevations of GRSA would also be useful.

# 6.0 Literature Cited

Abbs, D. J., and R. A. Pielke. 1987. Numerical simulations of orographic effects on NE Colorado snowstorms. Meteorology and Atmospheric Physics **37**:1-10.

Adams, D. K., and A. C. Comrie. 1997. The North American Monsoon. Bulletin of the American Meteorological Society, **78**:2197-2213.

Agee, J. K. 1997. The severe weather wildfire - too hot to handle? Northwest Science **71**:153-156.

American Association of State Climatologists. 1985. Heights and exposure standards for sensors on automated weather stations. The State Climatologist **9**.

Arno, S. F. 1980. Forest fire history in the Northern Rockies. Journal of Forestry **78**:460-465.

Barnston, A. G., and R. E. Livezey. 1987. Classification, seasonality and persistence of low-frequency atmospheric circulation patterns. Monthly Weather Review **115**:1083-1126.

Bevis, M., S. Businger, T. A. Herring, C. Rocken, R. A. Anthes, and R. H. Ware. 1992. GPS meteorology: remote sensing of the atmospheric water vapor using the global positioning system. Journal of Geophysical Research **97**:75–94.

Bonan, G. B. 2002. Ecological Climatology: Concepts and Applications. Cambridge University Press.

Borchert, J. R. 1950. The climate of the central North American grassland. Annals of the Association of American Geographers **40**:1-3

Britten, M., E. W. Schweiger, B. Frakes, D. Manier, and D. Pillmore. 2005. Rocky Mountain Network Vital Signs Monitoring Plan: Phase II Report. Inventory and Monitoring Program, National Park Service: Fort Collins, Colorado.

Bureau of Land Management. 1997. Remote Automatic Weather Station (RAWS) and Remote Environmental Monitoring Systems (REMS) standards. RAWS/REMS Support Facility, Boise, Idaho.

Cayan, D. R., M. D. Dettinger, H. F Diaz, and N. E. Graham. 1998. Decadal variability of precipitation over western North America. Journal of Climate **11**:3148-3166.

Chapin III, F. S., M. S. Torn, and M. Tateno. 1996. Principles of ecosystem sustainability. The American Naturalist **148**:1016-1037.

D'Antonio, C. M. 2000. Fire, plant invasions, and global changes. Pages 65-93 *in* Mooney, H. A. and R. J. Hobbs, editors. Invasive species in a changing world. Island Press, Washington, D.C.

Daly, C., R. P. Neilson, and D. L. Phillips. 1994. A statistical-topographic model for mapping climatological precipitation over mountainous terrain. Journal of Applied Meteorology **33**:140-158.

Daly, C., W. P. Gibson, G. H. Taylor, G. L. Johnson, and P. Pasteris. 2002. A knowledge-based approach to the statistical mapping of climate. Climate Research **22**:99-113.

Doggett, M., C. Daly, J. Smith, W. Gibson, G. Taylor, G. Johnson, and P. Pasteris. 2004. High-resolution 1971-2000 mean monthly temperature maps for the western United States. Fourteenth AMS Conf. on Applied Climatology, 84th AMS Annual Meeting. Seattle, Washington, American Meteorological Society, Boston, Massachusetts, January 2004, Paper 4.3, CD-ROM.

Duan, J., M. Bevis, P. Fang, Y. Bock, S. Chiswell, S. Businger, C. Rocken, F. Solheim, T. van Hove, R. Ware, and others. 1996. GPS meteorology: direct estimation of the absolute value of precipitable water. Journal of Applied Meteorology **35**:830-838.

Environmental Protection Agency. 1987. On-site meteorological program guidance for regulatory modeling applications. EPA-450/4-87-013. Environmental Protection Agency, Office of Air Quality Planning and Standards, Research Triangle Park, North Carolina.

Finklin, A. I., and W. C. Fischer. 1990. Weather station handbook –an interagency guide for wildland managers. NFES No. 2140. National Wildfire Coordinating Group, Boise, Idaho.

Fischer, W. C. and A. F. Bradley. 1987. Fire ecology of western Montana forest habitat types. USDA Forest Service, Intermountain Research Station, General Technical Report, INT-223.

Frank, D. A. and S. J. McNaughton. 1992. The ecology of plants, large mammalian herbivores and drought in Yellowstone National Park. Ecology **73**:2043-2058.

Gabriel, H. W. 1976. Wilderness ecology: the Danaher Creek drainage, Bob Marshall Wilderness, Montana. Dissertation, The University of Montana, Missoula, Montana.

Gibson, W. P., C. Daly, T. Kittel, D. Nychka, C. Johns, N. Rosenbloom, A. McNab, and G. Taylor. 2002. Development of a 103-year high-resolution climate data set for the conterminous United States. Thirteenth AMS Conf. on Applied Climatology. Portland, Oregon, American Meteorological Society, Boston, MA, May 2002:181-183.

Hadley, J. L., and W. K. Smith. 1986. Wind effects on needles of timberline conifers: Seasonal influence on mortality. Ecology **67**:12-19.

Hessl, A. E., D. McKenzie, and R. Schellhaas. 2004. Drought and Pacific Decadal Oscillation linked to fire occurrence in the inland Pacific Northwest. Ecological Applications **14**:425-442.

Heyerdahl, E. K., L. B. Brubaker, and J. K. Agee. 2002. Annual and decadal climate forcing of historical fire regimes in the interior Pacific Northwest, USA. The Holocene **12**:597-604.

I&M. 2006. I&M Inventories home page. http://science.nature.nps.gov/im/inventory/index.cfm.

Jacobson, M. C., R. J. Charlson, H. Rodhe, and G. H. Orians. 2000. Earth System Science: From Biogeochemical Cycles to Global Change. Academic Press, San Diego.

Karl, T. R., V. E. Derr, D. R. Easterling, C. K. Folland, D. J. Hoffman, S. Levitus, N. Nicholls, D. E. Parker, and G. W. Withee. 1996. Critical issues for long-term climate monitoring. Pages 55-92 *in* T. R. Karl, editor. Long Term Climate Monitoring by the Global Climate Observing System, Kluwer Publishing.

Logan, J. A., and J. A. Powell. 2001. Ghost forests, global warming, and the mountain pine beetle. American Entomologist **47**:160-172.

Maddux, R. A. 1978. Comparison of meteorological aspects of the Big Thompson and Rapid City flash floods. Monthly Weather Review **106**:375-389.

Mantua, N. J. 2000. The Pacific Decadal Oscillation and climate forecasting for North America. Online. (http://www.atmos.washington.edu/~mantua/REPORTS/PDO/PDO_cs.htm) Accessed 27 April 2004.

Mantua, N. J. and S. R. Hare. 2002. The Pacific decadal oscillation. Journal of Oceanography **58**:35-44.

McKenzie, D., Z. Gedalof, D. L. Peterson, and P. Mote. 2004. Climate change, wildfire, and conservation. Conservation Biology **18**:890-902.

Mock, C. J. 1996. Climatic controls and spatial variations of precipitation in the Western United States. Journal of Climate **9**:1111-1125.

Mote, P. W., A. F. Hamlet, M. P. Clark, and D. P. Lettenmaier. 2005. Declining mountain snowpack in western North America. Bulletin of the American Meteorological Society **86**:39-49.

National Assessment Synthesis Team. 2001. Climate Change Impacts on the United States: The Potential Consequences of Climate Variability and Change, Report for the U.S. Global Change Research Program. Cambridge University Press, Cambridge, UK.

National Research Council. 2001. A Climate Services Vision: First Steps Toward the Future. National Academies Press, Washington, D.C.

National Wildfire Coordinating Group. 2004. National fire danger rating system weather station standards. Report PMS 426.3. National Wildfire Coordinating Group, Boise, Idaho.

Neilson, R. P. 1987. Biotic regionalization and climatic controls in western North America. Vegetatio **70**:135-147.

Oakley, K. L., L. P. Thomas, and S. G. Fancy. 2003. Guidelines for long-term monitoring protocols. Wildlife Society Bulletin **31**:1000-1003.

Petersen, W. A., L. D. Carey, S. A. Rutledge, J. C. Knievel, N. J. Doesken, R. H. Johnson, T. B. McKee, T. Vonder Haar, and J. F. Weaver. 1999. Mesoscale and radar observations of the Fort Collins flash flood of 28 July 1997. Bulletin of the American Meteorological Society, **80**:191-216.

Pfister, R. D., B. L. Kovalchik, S. F. Arno, and R. C. Presby. 1977. Forest habitat types of Montana. USDA Forest Service, Intermountain Forest and Range Experiment Station. General Technical Report INT-34.

Redmond, K. T., D. B. Simeral, and G. D. McCurdy. 2005. Climate monitoring for southwest Alaska national parks: network design and site selection. Report 05-01. Western Regional Climate Center, Reno, Nevada.

Redmond, K. T., and R. W. Koch. 1991. Surface climate and streamflow variability in the western United States and their relationship to large-scale circulation indices. Water Resources Research **27**:2381-2399.

Rodriguez-Iturbe, I. 2000. Ecohydrology: A hydrologic perspective of climate-soil-vegetation dynamics. Water Resources Research **36**:3-9.

Ropelewski, C. F., D. S. Gutzler, R. W. Higgins, and C. R. Mechoso. 2005. The North American Monsoon System. Naval Postgraduate School, School of Engineering and Applied Sciences. Regional Monsoon Topics, Review Topic A-4. 12 pp.

Schlesinger, W. H. 1997. Biogeochemistry: An Analysis of Global Change. Academic Press, San Diego.

Smith, J. K., and W. C. Fischer. 1997. Fire ecology of the forest habitat types of northern Idaho. USDA Forest Service, Intermountain Research Station, General Technical Report, INT-GTR-363.

Tanner, B. D. 1990. Automated weather stations. Remote Sensing Reviews **5**:73-98.

Tranquillini, W. 1979. Physiological ecology of the alpine timberline. Springer-Verlag, New York.

Wagner, F. H., R. Angell, M. Hahn, T. Lawlor, R. Tausch, and D. Toweill. 2003. Natural ecosystems III. The Great Basin. Pages 207-240 *in* F. H. Wagner, ed. Rocky Mountain/Great Basin regional climate-change assessment. Report for the U. S. global change research program. Utah State University, Logan, Utah.

Wallace, J. M., and D. S. Gutzler. 1981. Teleconnections in the geopotential height field during the Northern Hemisphere winter. Monthly Weather Review **109**:784-812.

Whitlock, C., S. L. Shafer, and J. Marlon. 2003. The role of climate and vegetation change in shaping past and future fire regimes in the northwestern US and the implications for ecosystem management. Forest Ecology and Management **178**:5-21.

World Meteorological Organization. 1983. Guide to meteorological instruments and methods of observation, No. 8, 5th edition, World Meteorological Organization, Geneva Switzerland.

World Meteorological Organization. 2005. Organization and planning of intercomparisons of rainfall intensity gauges. World Meteorological Organization, Geneva Switzerland.

Yuan, L. L., R. A. Anthes, R. H. Ware, C. Rocken, W. D. Bonner, M. G. Bevis, and S. Businger. 1993. Sensing climate change using the global positioning system. Journal of Geophysical Research **98**:14925-14937.

Ziemer, R. R. and T. E. Lisle. 1998. Hydrology. *In* R. J. Naiman and R. E. Bilby, editors. River ecology and management: lessons from the Pacific Coastal Ecoregion. Springer-Verlag, New York, New York.

# Appendix A. Glossary

**Climate**—Complete and entire ensemble of statistical descriptors of temporal and spatial properties comprising the behavior of the atmosphere. These descriptors include means, variances, frequency distributions, autocorrelations, spatial correlations and other patterns of association, temporal lags, and element-to-element relationships. The descriptors have a physical basis in flows and reservoirs of energy and mass. Climate and weather phenomena shade gradually into each other and are ultimately inseparable.

**Climate Element**—(same as Weather Element) Attribute or property of the state of the atmosphere that is measured, estimated, or derived. Examples of climate elements include temperature, wind speed, wind direction, precipitation amount, precipitation type, relative humidity, dewpoint, solar radiation, snow depth, soil temperature at a given depth, etc. A derived element is a function of other elements (like degree days or number of days with rain) and is not measured directly with a sensor. The terms "parameter" or "variable" are not used to describe elements.

**Climate Network**—Group of climate stations having a common purpose; the group is often owned and maintained by a single organization.

**Climate Station**—Station where data are collected to track atmospheric conditions over the long-term. Often, this station operates to additional standards to verify long-term consistency. For these stations, the detailed circumstances surrounding a set of measurements (siting and exposure, instrument changes, etc.) are important.

**Data**—Measurements specifying the state of the physical environment. Does not include metadata.

**Data Inventory**—Information about overall data properties for each station within a weather or climate network. A data inventory may include start/stop dates, percentages of available data, breakdowns by climate element, counts of actual data values, counts or fractions of data types, etc. These properties must be determined by actually reading the data and thus require the data to be available, accessible, and in a readable format.

**NPS I&M Network**—A set of NPS park units grouped by a common theme, typically by natural resource and/or geographic region.

**Metadata**—Information necessary to interpret environmental data properly, organized as a history or series of snapshots—data about data. Examples include details of measurement processes, station circumstances and exposures, assumptions about the site, network purpose and background, types of observations and sensors, pre-treatment of data, access information, maintenance history and protocols, observational methods, archive locations, owner, and station start/end period.

**Quality Assurance**—Planned and systematic set of activities to provide adequate confidence that products and services are resulting in credible and correct information. Includes quality control.

**Quality Control**—Evaluation, assessment, and improvement of imperfect data by utilizing other imperfect data.

**Station Inventory**—Information about a set of stations obtained from metadata that accompany the network or networks. A station inventory can be compiled from direct and indirect reports prepared by others.

**Weather**—Instantaneous state of the atmosphere at any given time, mainly with respect to its effects on biological activities. As distinguished from climate, weather consists of the short-term (minutes to days) variations in the atmosphere. Popularly, weather is thought of in terms of temperature, precipitation, humidity, wind, sky condition, visibility, and cloud conditions.

**Weather Element** (same as Climate Element)—Attribute or property of the state of the atmosphere that is measured, estimated, or derived. Examples of weather elements include temperature, wind speed, wind direction, precipitation amount, precipitation type, relative humidity, dewpoint, solar radiation, snow depth, soil temperature at a given depth, etc. A derived weather element is a function of other elements (like degree days or number of days with rain) and is not measured directly. The terms "parameter" and "variable" are not used to describe weather elements.

**Weather Network**—Group of weather stations usually owned and maintained by a particular organization and usually for a specific purpose.

**Weather Station**—Station where collected data are intended for near-real-time use with less need for reference to long-term conditions. In many cases, the detailed circumstances of a set of measurements (siting and exposure, instrument changes, etc.) from weather stations are not as important as for climate stations.

# Appendix B. Climate-monitoring principles

Since the late 1990s, frequent references have been made to a set of climate-monitoring principles enunciated in 1996 by Tom Karl, director of the NOAA NCDC in Asheville, North Carolina. These monitoring principles also have been referred to informally as the "Ten Commandments of Climate Monitoring." Both versions are given here. In addition, these principles have been adopted by the Global Climate Observing System (GCOS 2004).

(Compiled by Kelly Redmond, Western Regional Climate Center, Desert Research Institute, August 2000.)

## B.1. Full Version (Karl et al. 1996)

***B.1.1.*** Effects on climate records of instrument changes, observing practices, observation locations, sampling rates, etc., must be known before such changes are implemented. This can be ascertained through a period where overlapping measurements from old and new observing systems are collected or sometimes by comparing the old and new observing systems with a reference standard. Site stability for in situ measurements, both in terms of physical location and changes in the nearby environment, also should be a key criterion in site selection. Thus, many synoptic network stations, which are primarily used in weather forecasting but also provide valuable climate data, and dedicated climate stations intended to be operational for extended periods must be subject to this policy.

***B.1.2.*** Processing algorithms and changes in these algorithms must be well documented. Documentation should be carried with the data throughout the data-archiving process.

***B.1.3.*** Knowledge of instrument, station, and/or platform history is essential for interpreting and using the data. Changes in instrument sampling time, local environmental conditions for in situ measurements, and other factors pertinent to interpreting the observations and measurements should be recorded as a mandatory part in the observing routine and be archived with the original data.

***B.1.4.*** In situ and other observations with a long, uninterrupted record should be maintained. Every effort should be applied to protect the data sets that have provided long-term, homogeneous observations. "Long-term" for space-based measurements is measured in decades, but for more conventional measurements, "long-term" may be a century or more. Each element in the observational system should develop a list of prioritized sites or observations based on their contribution to long-term climate monitoring.

***B.1.5.*** Calibration, validation, and maintenance facilities are critical requirements for long-term climatic data sets. Homogeneity in the climate record must be assessed routinely, and corrective action must become part of the archived record.

***B.1.6.*** Where feasible, some level of "low-technology" backup to "high-technology" observing systems should be developed to safeguard against unexpected operational failures.

***B.1.7.*** Regions having insufficient data, variables and regions sensitive to change, and key measurements lacking adequate spatial and temporal resolution should be given the highest priority in designing and implementing new climate-observing systems.

***B.1.8.*** Network designers and instrument engineers must receive long-term climate requirements at the outset of the network design process. This is particularly important because most observing systems have been designed for purposes other than long-term climate monitoring. Instruments must possess adequate accuracy with biases small enough to document climate variations and changes.

***B.1.9.*** Much of the development of new observational capabilities and the evidence supporting the value of these observations stem from research-oriented needs or programs. A lack of stable, long-term commitment to these observations and lack of a clear transition plan from research to operations are two frequent limitations in the development of adequate, long-term monitoring capabilities. Difficulties in securing a long-term commitment must be overcome in order to improve the climate-observing system in a timely manner with minimal interruptions.

***B.1.10.*** Data management systems that facilitate access, use, and interpretation are essential. Freedom of access, low cost, mechanisms that facilitate use (directories, catalogs, browse capabilities, availability of metadata on station histories, algorithm accessibility and documentation, etc.) and quality control should guide data management. International cooperation is critical for successful management of data used to monitor long-term climate change and variability.

## B.2. Abbreviated version, "Ten Commandments of Climate Monitoring"
***B.2.1.*** Assess the impact of new climate-observing systems or changes to existing systems before they are implemented.

"Thou shalt properly manage network change." (assess effects of proposed changes)

***B.2.2.*** Require a suitable period where measurement from new and old climate-observing systems will overlap.

"Thou shalt conduct parallel testing." (compare old and replacement systems)

***B.2.3.*** Treat calibration, validation, algorithm-change, and data-homogeneity assessments with the same care as the data.

"Thou shalt collect metadata." (fully document system and operating procedures)

***B.2.4.*** Verify capability for routinely assessing the quality and homogeneity of the data including high-resolution data for extreme events.

"Thou shalt assure data quality and continuity." (assess as part of routine operating procedures)

***B.2.5.*** Integrate assessments like those conducted by the International Panel on Climate Change into global climate-observing priorities.

"Thou shalt anticipate the use of data." (integrated environmental assessment; component in operational plan for system)

*B.2.6.* Maintain long-term weather and climate stations.

"Thou shalt worship historic significance." (maintain homogeneous data sets from long–term, climate-observing systems)

*B.2.7.* Place high priority on increasing observations in regions lacking sufficient data and in regions sensitive to change and variability.

"Thou shalt acquire complementary data." (new sites to fill observational gaps)

*B.2.8.* Provide network operators, designers, and instrument engineers with long-term requirements at the outset of the design and implementation phases for new systems.

"Thou shalt specify requirements for climate observation systems." (application and usage of observational data)

*B.2.9.* Carefully consider the transition from research-observing system to long-term operation.

"Thou shalt have continuity of purpose." (stable long-term commitments)

*B.2.10.* Focus on data-management systems that facilitate access, use, and interpretation of weather data and metadata.

"Thou shalt provide access to data and metadata." (readily available weather and climate information)

## B.3. Literature Cited

Karl, T. R., V. E. Derr, D. R. Easterling, C. K. Folland, D. J. Hoffman, S. Levitus, N. Nicholls, D. E. Parker, and G. W. Withee. 1996. Critical Issues for Long-Term Climate Monitoring. Pages 55-92 *in* T. R. Karl, editor. Long Term Climate Monitoring by the Global Climate Observing System, Kluwer Publishing.

Global Climate Observing System. 2004. Implementation Plan for the Global Observing System for Climate in Support of the UNFCCC. GCOS-92, WMO/TD No. 1219, World Meteorological Organization, Geneva, Switzerland.

# Appendix C. Factors in operating a weather/ climate network

## C.1. Climate versus Weather

- Climate measurements require *consistency through time.*

## C.2. Network Purpose

- Anticipated or desired lifetime.
- Breadth of network mission (commitment by needed constituency).
- Dedicated constituency—no network survives without a dedicated constituency.

## C.3. Site Identification and Selection

- Spanning gradients in climate or biomes with transects.
- Issues regarding representative spatial scale—site uniformity versus site clustering.
- Alignment with and contribution to network mission.
- Exposure—ability to measure representative quantities.
- Logistics—ability to service station (Always or only in favorable weather?).
- Site redundancy (positive for quality control, negative for extra resources).
- Power—is AC needed?
- Site security—is protection from vandalism needed?
- Permitting often a major impediment and usually underestimated.

## C.4. Station Hardware

- Survival—weather is the main cause of lost weather/climate data.
- Robustness of sensors—ability to measure and record in any condition.
- Quality—distrusted records are worthless and a waste of time and money.
  - High quality—will cost up front but pays off later.
  - Low quality—may provide a lower start-up cost but will cost more later (low cost can be expensive).
- Redundancy—backup if sensors malfunction.
- Ice and snow—measurements are much more difficult than rain measurements.
- Severe environments (expense is about two–three times greater than for stations in more benign settings).

## C.5. Communications

- Reliability—live data have a much larger constituency.
- One-way or two-way.
  - Retrieval of missed transmissions.
  - Ability to reprogram data logger remotely.
  - Remote troubleshooting abilities.
  - Continuing versus one-time costs.
- Back-up procedures to prevent data loss during communication outages.
- Live communications increase problems but also increase value.

## C.6. Maintenance

- Main reason why networks fail (and most networks do eventually fail!).
- <u>Key</u> issue with nearly every network.
- Who will perform maintenance?
- Degree of commitment and motivation to contribute.
- Periodic? On-demand as needed? Preventive?
- Equipment change-out schedules and upgrades for sensors and software.
- Automated stations require <u>skilled</u> and <u>experienced</u> labor.
- Calibration—sensors often drift (climate).
- Site maintenance essential (constant vegetation, surface conditions, nearby influences).
- Typical automated station will cost about $2K per year to maintain.
- Documentation—photos, notes, visits, changes, essential for posterity.
- Planning for equipment life cycle and technological advances.

## C.7. Maintaining Programmatic Continuity and Corporate Knowledge

- Long-term vision and commitment needed.
- Institutionalizing versus personalizing—developing appropriate dependencies.

## C.8. Data Flow

- Centralized ingest?
- Centralized access to data and data products?
- Local version available?
- Contract out work or do it yourself?
- Quality control of data.
- Archival.
- Metadata—historic information, not a snapshot. Every station should collect metadata.
- Post-collection processing, multiple data-ingestion paths.

## C.9. Products

- Most basic product consists of the data values.
- Summaries.
- Write own applications or leverage existing mechanisms?

## C.10. Funding

- Prototype approaches as proof of concept.
- Linking and leveraging essential.
- Constituencies—every network <u>needs</u> a constituency.
- Bridging to practical and operational communities? Live data needed.
- Bridging to counterpart research efforts and initiatives—funding source.
- Creativity, resourcefulness, and persistence usually are essential to success.

## C.11. Final Comments

- Deployment is by far the easiest part in operating a network.
- Maintenance is the main issue.
- Best analogy: Operating a network is like raising a child; it requires constant attention.

Source: Western Regional Climate Center (WRCC)

# Appendix D. General design considerations for weather/climate-monitoring programs

The process for designing a climate-monitoring program benefits from anticipating design and protocol issues discussed here. Much of this material is been excerpted from a report addressing the Channel Islands National Park (Redmond and McCurdy 2005), where an example is found illustrating how these factors can be applied to a specific setting. Many national park units possess some climate or meteorology feature that sets them apart from more familiar or "standard" settings.

## D.1. Introduction
There are several criteria that must be used in deciding to deploy new stations and where these new stations should be sited.

- Where are existing stations located?
- Where have data been gathered in the past (discontinued locations)?
- Where would a new station fill a knowledge gap about basic, long-term climatic averages for an area of interest?
- Where would a new station fill a knowledge gap about how climate behaves over time?
- As a special case for behavior over time, what locations might be expected to show a more sensitive response to climate change?
- How do answers to the preceding questions depend on the climate element? Are answers the same for precipitation, temperature, wind, snowfall, humidity, etc.?
- What role should manual measurements play? How should manual measurements interface with automated measurements?
- Are there special technical or management issues, either present or anticipated in the next 5–15 years, requiring added climate information?
- What unique information is provided in addition to information from existing sites? "Redundancy is bad."
- What nearby information is available to estimate missing observations because observing systems always experience gaps and lose data? "Redundancy is good."
- How would logistics and maintenance affect these decisions?

In relation to the preceding questions, there are several topics that should be considered. The following topics are not listed in a particular order.

### D.1.1. Network Purpose
Humans seem to have an almost reflexive need to measure temperature and precipitation, along with other climate elements. These reasons span a broad range from utilitarian to curiosity-driven. Although there are well-known recurrent patterns of need and data use, new uses are always appearing. The number of uses ranges in the thousands. Attempts have been made to categorize such uses (see NRC 1998; NRC 2001). Because climate measurements are accumulated over a long time, they should be treated as multi-purpose and should be undertaken in a manner that serves the widest possible applications. Some applications remain constant, while others rise and fall in importance. An insistent issue today may subside, while the next pressing issue of tomorrow barely may be anticipated. The notion that humans might affect the

climate of the entire Earth was nearly unimaginable when the national USDA (later NOAA) cooperative weather network began in the late 1800s. Abundant experience has shown, however, that there always will be a demand for a history record of climate measurements and their properties. Experience also shows that there is an expectation that climate measurements will be taken and made available to the general public.

An exhaustive list of uses for data would fill many pages and still be incomplete. In broad terms, however, there are needs to document environmental conditions that disrupt or otherwise affect park operations (e.g., storms and droughts). Design and construction standards are determined by climatological event frequencies that exceed certain thresholds. Climate is a determinant that sometimes attracts and sometimes discourages visitors. Climate may play a large part in the park experience (e.g., Death Valley and heat are nearly synonymous). Some park units are large enough to encompass spatial or elevation diversity in climate and the sequence of events can vary considerably inside or close to park boundaries. That is, temporal trends and statistics may not be the same everywhere, and this spatial structure should be sampled. The granularity of this structure depends on the presence of topography or large climate gradients or both, such as that found along the U.S. West Coast in summer with the rapid transition from the marine layer to the hot interior.

Plant and animal communities and entire ecosystems react to every nuance in the physical environment. No aspect of weather and climate goes undetected in the natural world. Wilson (1998) proposed "an informal rule of biological evolution" that applies here: "If an organic sensor can be imagined that is capable of detecting any particular environmental signal, a species exists somewhere that possesses this sensor." Every weather and climate event, whether dull or extraordinary to humans, matters to some organism. Dramatic events and creeping incremental change both have consequences to living systems. Extreme events or disturbances can "reset the clock" or "shake up the system" and lead to reverberations that last for years to centuries or longer. Slow change can carry complex nonlinear systems (e.g., any living assemblage) into states where chaotic transitions and new behavior occur. These changes are seldom predictable, typically are observed after the fact, and understood only in retrospect. Climate changes may not be exciting, but as a well-known atmospheric scientist, Mike Wallace, from the University of Washington once noted, "subtle does not mean unimportant."

Thus, individuals who observe the climate should be able to record observations accurately and depict both rapid and slow changes. In particular, an array of artificial influences easily can confound detection of slow changes. The record as provided can contain both real climate variability (that took place in the atmosphere) and fake climate variability (that arose directly from the way atmospheric changes were observed and recorded). As an example, trees growing near a climate station with an excellent anemometer will make it appear that the wind gradually slowed down over many years. Great care must be taken to protect against sources of fake climate variability on the longer-time scales of years to decades. Processes leading to the observed climate are not stationary; rather these processes draw from probability distributions that vary with time. For this reason, climatic time series do not exhibit statistical stationarity. The implications are manifold. There are no true climatic "normals" to which climate inevitably must return. Rather, there are broad ranges of climatic conditions. Climate does not demonstrate exact repetition but instead continual fluctuation and sometimes approximate repetition. In addition, there is always new behavior waiting to occur. Consequently, the business of climate monitoring is never finished, and there is no point where we can state confidently that "enough" is known.

### D.1.2. Robustness
The most frequent cause for loss of weather data is the weather itself, the very thing we wish to record. The design of climate and weather observing programs should consider the meteorological equivalent of "peaking power" employed by utilities. Because environmental disturbances have significant effects on ecologic systems, sensors, data loggers, and communications networks should be able to function during the most severe conditions that realistically can be anticipated over the next 50–100 years. Systems designed in this manner are less likely to fail under more ordinary conditions, as well as more likely to transmit continuous, quality data for both tranquil and active periods.

### D.1.3. Weather versus Climate
For "weather" measurements, pertaining to what is approximately happening here and now, small moves and changes in exposure are not as critical. For "climate" measurements, where values from different points in time are compared, siting and exposure are critical factors, and it is vitally important that the observing circumstances remain essentially unchanged over the duration of the station record.

Station moves can affect different elements to differing degrees. Even small moves of several meters, especially vertically, can affect temperature records. Hills and knolls act differently from the bottoms of small swales, pockets, or drainage channels (Whiteman 2000; Geiger et al. 2003). Precipitation is probably less subject to change with moves of 50–100 m than other elements (that is, precipitation has less intrinsic variation in small spaces) except if wind flow over the gauge is affected.

### D.1.4. Physical Setting
Siting and exposure, and their continuity and consistency through time, significantly influence the climate records produced by a station. These two terms have overlapping connotations. We use the term "siting" in a more general sense, reserving the term "exposure" generally for the particular circumstances affecting the ability of an instrument to record measurements that are representative of the desired spatial or temporal scale.

### D.1.5. Measurement Intervals
Climatic processes occur continuously in time, but our measurement systems usually record in discrete chunks of time: for example, seconds, hours, or days. These measurements often are referred to as "systematic" measurements. Interval averages may hide active or interesting periods of highly intense activity. Alternatively, some systems record "events" when a certain threshold of activity is exceeded (examples: another millimeter of precipitation has fallen, another kilometer of wind has moved past, the temperature has changed by a degree, a gust higher than 9.9 m/s has been measured). When this occurs, measurements from all sensors are reported. These measurements are known as "breakpoint" data. In relatively unchanging conditions (long calm periods or rainless weeks, for example), event recorders should send a signal that they are still "alive and well." If systematic recorders are programmed to note and periodically report the highest, lowest, and mean value within each time interval, the likelihood

is reduced that interesting behavior will be glossed over or lost. With the capacity of modern data loggers, it is recommended to record and report extremes within the basic time increment (e.g., hourly or 10 minutes). This approach also assists quality-control procedures.

There is usually a trade-off between data volume and time increment, and most automated systems now are set to record approximately hourly. A number of field stations maintained by WRCC are programmed to record in 5- or 10-minute increments, which readily serve to construct an hourly value. However, this approach produces 6–12 times as much data as hourly data. These systems typically do not record details of events at sub-interval time scales, but they easily can record peak values, or counts of threshold exceedance, within the time intervals.

Thus, for each time interval at an automated station, we recommend that several kinds of information—mean or sum, extreme maximum and minimum, and sometimes standard deviation—be recorded. These measurements are useful for quality control and other purposes. Modern data loggers and office computers have quite high capacity. Diagnostic information indicating the state of solar chargers or battery voltages and their extremes is of great value. This topic will be discussed in greater detail in a succeeding section.

Automation also has made possible adaptive or intelligent monitoring techniques where systems vary the recording rate based on detection of the behavior of interest by the software. Sub-interval behavior of interest can be masked on occasion (e.g., a 5-minute extreme downpour with high-erosive capability hidden by an innocuous hourly total). Most users prefer measurements that are systematic in time because they are much easier to summarize and manipulate.

For breakpoint data produced by event reporters, there also is a need to send periodically a signal that the station is still functioning, even though there is nothing more to report. "No report" does not necessarily mean "no data," and it is important to distinguish between the actual observation that was recorded and the content of that observation (e.g., an observation of "0.00" is not the same as "no observation").

### D.1.6. Mixed Time Scales
There are times when we may wish to combine information from radically different scales. For example, over the past 100 years we may want to know how the frequency of 5-minute precipitation peaks has varied or how the frequency of peak 1-second wind gusts have varied. We may also want to know over this time if nearby vegetation gradually has grown up to increasingly block the wind or to slowly improve precipitation catch. Answers to these questions require knowledge over a wide range of time scales.

### D.1.7. Elements
For manual measurements, the typical elements recorded included temperature extremes, precipitation, and snowfall/snow depth. Automated measurements typically include temperature, precipitation, humidity, wind speed and direction, and solar radiation. An exception to this exists in very windy locations where precipitation is difficult to measure accurately. Automated measurements of snow are improving, but manual measurements are still preferable, as long as shielding is present. Automated measurement of frozen precipitation presents numerous challenges that have not been resolved fully, and the best gauges are quite expensive ($3–8K).

Soil temperatures also are included sometimes. Soil moisture is extremely useful, but measurements are not made at many sites. In addition, care must be taken in the installation and maintenance of instruments used in measuring soil moisture. Soil properties vary tremendously in short distances as well, and it is often very difficult ("impossible") to accurately document these variations (without digging up all the soil!). In cooler climates, ultrasonic sensors that detect snow depth are becoming commonplace.

### D.1.8. Wind Standards

Wind varies the most in the shortest distance, since it always decreases to zero near the ground and increases rapidly (approximately logarithmically) with height near the ground. Changes in anemometer height obviously will affect distribution of wind speed as will changes in vegetation, obstructions such as buildings, etc. A site that has a 3-m (10-ft) mast clearly will be less windy than a site that has a 6-m (20-ft) or 10-m (33-ft) mast. Historically, many U.S. airports (FAA and NWS) and most current RAWS sites have used a standard 6-m (20-ft) mast for wind measurements. Some NPS RAWS sites utilize shorter masts. Over the last decade, as Automated Surface Observing Systems (ASOSs, mostly NWS) and Automated Weather Observing Systems (AWOSs, mostly FAA) have been deployed at most airports, wind masts have been raised to 8 or 10 m (26 or 33 ft), depending on airplane clearance. The World Meteorological Organization recommends 10 m as the height for wind measurements (WMO 1983; 2005), and more groups are migrating slowly to this standard. The American Association of State Climatologists (AASC 1985) have recommended that wind be measured at 3 m, a standard geared more for agricultural applications than for general purpose uses where higher levels usually are preferred. Different anemometers have different starting thresholds; therefore, areas that frequently experience very light winds may not produce wind measurements thus affecting long-term mean estimates of wind speed. For both sustained winds (averages over a short interval of 2–60 minutes) and especially for gusts, the duration of the sampling interval makes a considerable difference. For the same wind history, 1–second gusts are higher than gusts averaging 3 seconds, which in turn are greater than 5-second averages, so that the same sequence would be described with different numbers (all three systems and more are in use). Changes in the averaging procedure, or in height or exposure, can lead to "false" or "fake" climate change with no change in actual climate. Changes in any of these should be noted in the metadata.

### D.1.9. Wind Nomenclature

Wind is a vector quantity having a direction and a speed. Directions can be two- or three-dimensional; they will be three-dimensional if the vertical component is important. In all common uses, winds always are denoted by the direction they blow *from* (north wind or southerly breeze). This convention exists because wind often brings weather, and thus our attention is focused upstream. However, this approach contrasts with the way ocean currents are viewed. Ocean currents usually are denoted by the direction they are moving *towards* (eastward current moves from west to east). In specialized applications (such as in atmospheric modeling), wind velocity vectors point in the direction that the wind is blowing. Thus, a southwesterly wind (from the southwest) has both northward and eastward (to the north and to the east) components. Except near mountains, wind cannot blow up or down near the ground, so the vertical component of wind often is approximated as zero, and the horizontal component is emphasized.

### D.1.10. Frozen Precipitation

Frozen precipitation is more difficult to measure than liquid precipitation, especially with automated techniques. Sevruk and Harmon (1984), Goodison et al. (1998), and Yang et al. (1998; 2001) provide many of the reasons to explain this. The importance of frozen precipitation varies greatly from one setting to another. This subject was discussed in greater detail in a related inventory and monitoring report for the Alaska park units (Redmond et al. 2005).

In climates that receive frozen precipitation, a decision must be made whether or not to try to record such events accurately. This usually means that the precipitation must be turned into liquid either by falling into an antifreeze fluid solution that is then weighed or by heating the precipitation enough to melt and fall through a measuring mechanism such as a nearly-balanced tipping bucket. Accurate measurements from the first approach require expensive gauges; tipping buckets can achieve this resolution readily but are more apt to lose some or all precipitation. Improvements have been made to the heating mechanism on the NWS tipping-bucket gauge used for the ASOS to correct its numerous deficiencies making it less problematic; however, this gauge is not inexpensive. A heat supply needed to melt frozen precipitation usually requires more energy than renewable energy (solar panels or wind recharging) can provide thus AC power is needed. Periods of frozen precipitation or rime often provide less-than-optimal recharging conditions with heavy clouds, short days, low-solar-elevation angles and more horizon blocking, and cold temperatures causing additional drain on the battery.

### D.1.11. Save or Lose

A second consideration with precipitation is determining if the measurement should be saved (as in weighing systems) or lost (as in tipping-bucket systems). With tipping buckets, after the water has passed through the tipping mechanism, it usually just drops to the ground. Thus, there is no checksum to ensure that the sum of all the tips adds up to what has been saved in a reservoir at some location. By contrast, the weighing gauges continually accumulate until the reservoir is emptied, the reported value is the total reservoir content (for example, the height of the liquid column in a tube), and the incremental precipitation is the difference in depth between two known times. These weighing gauges do not always have the same fine resolution. Some gauges only record to the nearest centimeter, which is usually acceptable for hydrology but not necessarily for other needs. (For reference, a millimeter of precipitation can get a person in street clothes quite wet.) Other weighing gauges are capable of measuring to the 0.25-mm (0.01-in.) resolution but do not have as much capacity and must be emptied more often. Day/night and storm-related thermal expansion and contraction and sometimes wind shaking can cause fluid pressure from accumulated totals to go up and down in SNOTEL gauges by small increments (commonly 0.3-3 cm, or 0.01–0.10 ft) leading to "negative precipitation" followed by similarly non-real light precipitation when, in fact, no change took place in the amount of accumulated precipitation.

### D.1.12. Time

Time should always be in local standard time (LST), and daylight savings time (DST) should never be used under any circumstances with automated equipment and timers. Using DST leads to one duplicate hour, one missing hour, and a season of displaced values, as well as needless confusion and a data-management nightmare. Absolute time, such as Greenwich Mean Time (GMT) or Coordinated Universal Time (UTC), also can be used because these formats are unambiguously translatable. Since measurements only provide information about what already *has* occurred or *is* occurring and not what *will* occur, they should always be assigned to the *ending time* of the associated interval with hour 24 marking the end of the last hour of the day. In this system, midnight always represents the end of the day, not the start. To demonstrate the importance of this differentiation, we have encountered situations where police officers seeking corroborating weather data could not recall whether the time on their crime report from a year ago was the starting midnight or the ending midnight! Station positions should be known to within a few meters, easily accomplished with GPS, so that time zones and solar angles can be determined accurately.

### D.1.13. Automated versus Manual

Most of this report has addressed automated measurements. Historically, most measurements are manual and typically collected once a day. In many cases, manual measurements continue because of habit, usefulness, and desire for continuity over time. Manual measurements are extremely useful and when possible should be encouraged. However, automated measurements are becoming more common. For either, it is important to record time in a logically consistent manner.

It should not be automatically assumed that newer data and measurements are "better" than older data or that manual data are "worse" than automated data. Older or simpler manual measurements are often of very high quality even if they sometimes are not in the most convenient digital format.

There is widespread desire to use automated systems to reduce human involvement. This is admirable and understandable, but every automated weather/climate station or network requires significant human attention and maintenance. A telling example concerns the Oklahoma Mesonet (see Brock et al. 1995, and bibliography at http://www.mesonet.ou.edu), a network of about 115 high–quality, automated meteorological stations spread over Oklahoma, where about 80 percent of the annual ($2–3M) budget is nonetheless allocated to humans with only about 20 percent allocated to equipment.

### D.1.14. Manual Conventions

Manual measurements typically are made once a day. Elements usually consist of maximum and minimum temperature, temperature at observation time, precipitation, snowfall, snow depth, and sometimes evaporation, wind, or other information. Since it is not actually known when extremes occurred, the only logical approach, and the nationwide convention, is to ascribe the entire measurement to the time-interval date and to enter it on the form in that way. For morning observers (for example, 8 am to 8 am), this means that the maximum temperature written for today often is from yesterday afternoon and sometimes the minimum temperature for the 24-hr period actually occurred yesterday morning. However, this is understood and expected. It is often a surprise to observers to see how many maximum temperatures do not occur in the afternoon and how many minimum temperatures do not occur in the predawn hours. This is especially true in environments that are colder, higher, northerly, cloudy, mountainous, or coastal. As long as this convention is strictly followed every day, it has been shown that truly excellent climate records can result (Redmond 1992). Manual observers should reset equipment only one time per day at the official observing time. Making more than one measurement a day is discouraged strongly; this practice results in a hybrid record that is too difficult to interpret. The only exception is for total daily snowfall. New snowfall can be measured up to four times per day with no observations closer than six hours. It is well known that more frequent measurement of snow increases the annual total because compaction is a continuous process.

Two main purposes for climate observations are to establish the long-term averages for given locations and to track variations in climate. Broadly speaking, these purposes address topics of absolute and relative climate behavior. Once absolute behavior has been "established" (a task that is never finished because long-term averages continue to vary in time)—temporal variability quickly becomes the item of most interest.

## D.2. Representativeness

Having discussed important factors to consider when new sites are installed, we now turn our attention to site "representativeness." In popular usage, we often encounter the notion that a site is "representative" of another site if it receives the same annual precipitation or records the same annual temperature or if some other element-specific, long-term average has a similar value. This notion of representativeness has a certain limited validity, but there are other aspects of this idea that need to be considered.

A climate monitoring site also can be said to be representative if climate records from that site show sufficiently strong temporal correlations with a large number of locations over a sufficiently large area. If station A receives 20 cm a year and station B receives 200 cm a year, these climates obviously receive quite differing amounts of precipitation. However, if their monthly, seasonal, or annual correlations are high (for example, 0.80 or higher for a particular time scale), one site can be used as a surrogate for estimating values at the other if measurements for a particular month, season, or year are missing. That is, a wet or dry month at one station is also a wet or dry month (relative to its own mean) at the comparison station. Note that high correlations on one time scale do not imply automatically that high correlations will occur on other time scales.

Likewise, two stations having similar mean climates (for example, similar annual precipitation) might not co-vary in close synchrony (for example, coastal versus interior). This may be considered a matter of climate "affiliation" for a particular location.

Thus, the representativeness of a site can refer either to the basic climatic averages for a given duration (or time window within the annual cycle) or to the extent that the site co-varies in time with respect to all surrounding locations. One site can be representative of another in the first sense but not the second, or vice versa, or neither, or both—all combinations are possible.

If two sites are perfectly correlated then, in a sense, they are "redundant." However, redundancy has value because all sites will experience missing data especially with automated equipment in rugged environments and harsh climates where outages and other problems nearly can be guaranteed. In many cases, those outages are caused by the weather, particularly by unusual weather and the very conditions we most wish to know about. Methods for filling in those values will require proxy information from this or other nearby networks. Thus, redundancy is a virtue rather than a vice.

In general, the cooperative stations managed by the NWS have produced much longer records than automated stations like RAWS or SNOTEL stations. The RAWS stations often have problems with precipitation, especially in winter, or with missing data, so that low correlations may be data problems rather than climatic dissimilarity. The RAWS records also are relatively short, so correlations should be interpreted with care. In performing and interpreting such analyses, however, we must remember that there are physical climate reasons and observational reasons why stations within a short distance (even a few tens or hundreds of meters) may not correlate well.

### D.2.1. Temporal Behavior

It is possible that high correlations will occur between station pairs during certain portions of the year (i.e., January) but low correlations may occur during other portions of the year (e.g., September or October). The relative contributions of these seasons to the annual total (for precipitation) or average (for temperature) and the correlations for each month are both factors in the correlation of an aggregated time window of longer duration that encompasses those seasons (e.g., one of the year definitions such as calendar year or water year). A complete and careful evaluation ideally would include such a correlation analysis but requires more resources and data. Note that it also is possible and frequently is observed that temperatures are highly correlated while precipitation is not or vice versa, and these relations can change according to the time of year. If two stations are well correlated for all climate elements for all portions of the year, then they can be considered redundant.

With scarce resources, the initial strategy should be to try to identify locations that do not correlate particularly well, so that each new site measures something new that cannot be guessed easily from the behavior of surrounding sites. (An important caveat here is that lack of such correlation could be a result of physical climate behavior and not a result of faults with the actual measuring process; i.e., by unrepresentative or simply poor-quality data. Unfortunately, we seldom have perfect climate data.) As additional sites are added, we usually wish for some combination of unique and redundant sites to meet what amounts to essentially orthogonal constraints: new information and more reliably-furnished information.

A common consideration is whether to observe on a ridge or in a valley, given the resources to place a single station within a particular area of a few square kilometers. Ridge and valley stations will correlate very well for temperatures when lapse conditions prevail, particularly summer daytime temperatures. In summer at night or winter at daylight, the picture will be more mixed and correlations will be lower. In winter at night when inversions are common and even the rule, correlations may be zero or even negative and perhaps even more divergent as the two sites are on opposite sides of the inversion. If we had the luxury of locating stations everywhere, we would find that ridge tops generally correlate very well with other ridge tops and similarly valleys with other valleys, but ridge tops correlate well with valleys only under certain circumstances. Beyond this, valleys and ridges having similar orientations usually will correlate better with each other than those with perpendicular orientations, depending on their orientation with respect to large-scale wind flow and solar angles.

Unfortunately, we do not have stations everywhere, so we are forced to use the few comparisons that we have and include a large dose of intelligent reasoning, using what we have observed elsewhere. In performing and interpreting such analyses, we must remember that there are physical climatic reasons and observational reasons why stations within a short distance (even a few tens or hundreds of meters) may not correlate well.

Examples of correlation analyses include those for the Channel Islands and for southwest Alaska, which can be found in Redmond and McCurdy (2005) and Redmond et al. (2005). These examples illustrate what can be learned from correlation analyses. Spatial correlations generally vary by time of year. Thus, results should be displayed in the form of annual correlation cycles— for monthly mean temperature and monthly total precipitation and perhaps other climate elements like wind or humidity—between station pairs selected for climatic setting and data availability and quality.

In general, the COOP stations managed by the NWS have produced much longer records than have automated stations like RAWS or SNOTEL stations. The RAWS stations also often have problems with precipitation, especially in winter or with missing data, so that low correlations may be data problems rather than climate dissimilarity. The RAWS records are much shorter, so correlations should be interpreted with care, but these stations are more likely to be in places of interest for remote or under-sampled regions.

### D.2.2. Spatial Behavior

A number of techniques exist to interpolate from isolated point values to a spatial domain. For example, a common technique is simple inverse distance weighting. Critical to the success of the simplest of such techniques is that some other property of the spatial domain, one that is influential for the mapped element, does not vary significantly. Topography greatly influences precipitation, temperature, wind, humidity, and most other meteorological elements. Thus, this criterion clearly is not met in any region having extreme topographic diversity. In such circumstances, simple Cartesian distance may have little to do with how rapidly correlation deteriorates from one site to the next, and in fact, the correlations can decrease readily from a mountain to a valley and then increase again on the next mountain. Such structure in the fields of spatial correlation is not seen in the relatively (statistically) well-behaved flat areas like those in the eastern U.S.

To account for dominating effects such as topography and inland–coastal differences that exist in certain regions, some kind of additional knowledge must be brought to bear to produce meaningful, physically plausible, and observationally based interpolations. Historically, this has proven to be an extremely difficult problem, especially to perform objective and repeatable analyses. An analysis performed for southwest Alaska (Redmond et al. 2005) concluded that the PRISM (Parameter Regression on Independent Slopes Model) maps (Daly et al. 1994; 2002; Gibson et al. 2002; Doggett et al. 2004) were probably the best available. An analysis by Simpson et al. (2005) further discussed many issues in the mapping of Alaska's climate and resulted in the same conclusion about PRISM.

### D.2.3. Climate-Change Detection

Although general purpose climate stations should be situated to address all aspects of climate variability, it is desirable that they also be in locations that are more sensitive to climate change from natural or anthropogenic influences should it begin to occur. The question here is how well we know such sensitivities. The climate-change issue is quite complex because it encompasses more than just greenhouse gasses.

Sites that are in locations or climates particularly vulnerable to climate change should be favored. How this vulnerability is determined is a considerably challenging research issue. Candidate locations or situations are those that lie on the border between two major biomes or just inside the edge of one or the other. In these cases, a slight movement of the boundary in anticipated direction (toward "warmer," for example) would be much easier to detect as the boundary moves past the site and a different set of biota begin to be established. Such a vegetative or ecologic response would be more visible and would take less time to establish as a real change than would a smaller change in the center of the distribution range of a marker or key species.

### D.2.4. Element-Specific Differences
The various climate elements (temperature, precipitation, cloudiness, snowfall, humidity, wind speed and direction, solar radiation) do not vary through time in the same sequence or manner nor should they necessarily be expected to vary in this manner. The spatial patterns of variability should not be expected to be the same for all elements. These patterns also should not be expected to be similar for all months or seasons. The suitability of individual sites for measurement also varies from one element to another. A site that has a favorable exposure for temperature or wind may not have a favorable exposure for precipitation or snowfall. A site that experiences proper air movement may be situated in a topographic channel, such as a river valley or a pass, which restricts the range of wind directions and affects the distribution of speed-direction categories.

### D.2.5. Logistics and Practical Factors
Even with the most advanced scientific rationale, sites in some remote or climatically challenging settings may not be suitable because of the difficulty in servicing and maintaining equipment. Contributing to these challenges are scheduling difficulties, animal behavior, snow burial, icing, snow behavior, access and logistical problems, and the weather itself. Remote and elevated sites usually require far more attention and expense than a rain-dominated, easily accessible valley location.

For climate purposes, station exposure and the local environment should be maintained in their original state (vegetation especially), so that changes seen are the result of regional climate variations and not of trees growing up, bushes crowding a site, surface albedo changing, fire clearing, etc. Repeat photography has shown many examples of slow environmental change in the vicinity of a station in rather short time frames (5–20 years), and this technique should be employed routinely and frequently at all locations. In the end, logistics, maintenance, and other practical factors almost always determine the success of weather- and climate-monitoring activities.

### D.2.6. Personnel Factors
Many past experiences (almost exclusively negative) strongly support the necessity to place primary responsibility for station deployment and maintenance in the hands of seasoned, highly qualified, trained, and meticulously careful personnel, the more experienced the better. Over

time, even in "benign" climates but especially where harsher conditions prevail, every conceivable problem will occur and both the usual and unusual should be anticipated: weather, animals, plants, salt, sensor and communication failure, windblown debris, corrosion, power failures, vibrations, avalanches, snow loading and creep, corruption of the data logger program, etc. An ability to anticipate and forestall such problems, a knack for innovation and improvisation, knowledge of electronics, practical and organizational skills, and presence of mind to bring the various small but vital parts, spares, tools, and diagnostic troubleshooting equipment are highly valued qualities. Especially when logistics are so expensive, a premium should be placed on using experienced personnel, since the slightest and seemingly most minor mistake can render a station useless or, even worse, uncertain. Exclusive reliance on individuals without this background can be costly and almost always will result eventually in unnecessary loss of data. Skilled labor and an apprenticeship system to develop new skilled labor will greatly reduce (but not eliminate) the types of problems that can occur in operating a climate network.

## D.3. Site Selection
In addition to considerations identified previously in this appendix, various factors need to be considered in selecting sites for new or augmented instrumentation.

### D.3.1. Equipment and Exposure Factors
D.3.1.1. Measurement Suite: All sites should measure temperature, humidity, wind, solar radiation, and snow depth. Precipitation measurements are more difficult but probably should be attempted with the understanding that winter measurements may be of limited or no value unless an all-weather gauge has been installed. Even if an all-weather gauge has been installed, it is desirable to have a second gauge present that operates on a different principle–for example, a fluid-based system like those used in the SNOTEL stations in tandem with a higher–resolution, tipping bucket gauge for summertime. Without heating, a tipping bucket gauge usually is of use only when temperatures are above freezing and when temperatures have not been below freezing for some time, so that accumulated ice and snow is not melting and being recorded as present precipitation. Gauge undercatch is a significant issue in snowy climates, so shielding should be considered for all gauges designed to work over the winter months. It is very important to note the presence or absence of shielding, the type of shielding, and the dates of installation or removal of the shielding.

D.3.1.2. Overall Exposure: The ideal, general all-purpose site has gentle slopes, is open to the sun and the wind, has a natural vegetative cover, avoids strong local (less than 200 m) influences, and represents a reasonable compromise among all climate elements. The best temperature sites are not the best precipitation sites, and the same is true for other elements. Steep topography in the immediate vicinity should be avoided unless settings where precipitation is affected by steep topography are being deliberately sought or a mountaintop or ridgeline is the desired location. The potential for disturbance should be considered: fire and flood risk, earth movement, wind-borne debris, volcanic deposits or lahars, vandalism, animal tampering, and general human encroachment are all factors.

D.3.1.3. Elevation: Mountain climates do not vary in time in exactly the same manner as adjoining valley climates. This concept is emphasized when temperature inversions are present to a greater degree and during precipitation when winds rise up the slopes at the same angle.

82

There is considerable concern that mountain climates will be (or already are) changing and perhaps changing differently than lowland climates, which has direct and indirect consequences for plant and animal life in the more extreme zones. Elevations of special significance are those that are near the mean rain/snow line for winter, near the tree line, and near the mean annual freezing level (all of these may not be quite the same). Because the lapse rates in wet climates often are nearly moist-adiabatic during the main precipitation seasons, measurements at one elevation may be extrapolated to nearby elevations. In drier climates and in the winter, temperature and to a lesser extent wind will show various elevation profiles.

D.3.1.4. Transects: The concept of observing transects that span climatic gradients is sound. This is not always straightforward in topographically uneven terrain, but these transects could still be arranged by setting up station(s) along the coast; in or near passes atop the main coastal interior drainage divide; and inland at one, two, or three distances into the interior lowlands. Transects need not—and by dint of topographic constraints probably cannot—be straight lines, but the closer that a line can be approximated the better. The main point is to systematically sample the key points of a behavioral transition without deviating too radically from linearity.

D.3.1.5. Other Topographic Considerations: There are various considerations with respect to local topography. Local topography can influence wind (channeling, upslope/downslope, etc.), precipitation (orographic enhancement, downslope evaporation, catch efficiency, etc.), and temperature (frost pockets, hilltops, aspect, mixing or decoupling from the overlying atmosphere, bowls, radiative effects, etc.), to different degrees at differing scales. In general, for measurements to be areally representative, it is better to avoid these local effects to the extent that they can be identified before station deployment (once deployed, it is desirable not to move a station). The primary purpose of a climate-monitoring network should be to serve as an infrastructure in the form of a set of benchmark stations for comparing other stations. Sometimes, however, it is exactly these local phenomena that we want to capture. Living organisms, especially plants, are affected by their immediate environment, whether it is representative of a larger setting or not. Specific measurements of limited scope and duration made for these purposes then can be tied to the main benchmarks. This experience is useful also in determining the complexity needed in the benchmark monitoring process in order to capture particular phenomena at particular space and time scales.

Sites that drain (cold air) well generally are better than sites that allow cold air to pool. Slightly sloped areas (1 degree is fine) or small benches from tens to hundreds of meters above streams are often favorable locations. Furthermore, these sites often tend to be out of the path of hazards (like floods) and to have rocky outcroppings where controlling vegetation will not be a major concern. Benches or wide spots on the rise between two forks of a river system are often the only flat areas and sometimes jut out to give greater exposure to winds from more directions.

D.3.1.6. Prior History: The starting point in designing a program is to determine what kinds of observations have been collected over time, by whom, in what manner, and if these observation are continuing to the present time. It also may be of value to "re-occupy" the former site of a station that is now inactive to provide some measure of continuity or a reference point from the past. This can be of value even if continuous observations were not made during the entire intervening period.

### D.3.2. Element-Specific Factors

D.3.2.1. Temperature: An open exposure with uninhibited air movement is the preferred setting. The most common measurement is made at approximately eye level, 1.5–2.0 m. In snowy locations sensors should be at least one meter higher than the deepest snowpack expected in the next 50 years or perhaps 2–3 times the depth of the average maximum annual depth. Sensors should be shielded above and below from solar radiation (bouncing off snow), from sunrise/sunset horizontal input, and from vertical rock faces. Sensors should be clamped tightly, so that they do not swivel away from level stacks of radiation plates. Nearby vegetation should be kept away from the sensors (several meters). Growing vegetation should be cut to original conditions. Small hollows and swales can cool tremendously at night, and it is best avoid these areas. Side slopes of perhaps a degree or two of angle facilitate air movement and drainage and, in effect, sample a large area during nighttime hours. The very bottom of a valley should be avoided. Temperature can change substantially from moves of only a few meters. Situations have been observed where flat and seemingly uniform conditions (like airport runways) appear to demonstrate different climate behaviors over short distances of a few tens or hundreds of meters (differences of 5–10°C). When snow is on the ground, these microclimatic differences can be stronger, and differences of 2–5°C can occur in the short distance between the thermometer and the snow surface on calm evenings.

D.3.2.2. Precipitation (liquid): Calm locations with vegetative or artificial shielding are preferred. Wind will adversely impact readings; therefore, the less the better. Wind effects on precipitation are far less for rain than for snow. Devices that "save" precipitation present advantages, but most gauges are built to dump precipitation as it falls or to empty periodically. Automated gauges give both the amount and the timing. Simple backups that record only the total precipitation since the last visit have a certain advantage (for example, storage gauges or lengths of PVC pipe perhaps with bladders on the bottom). The following question should be asked: Does the total precipitation from an automated gauge add up to the measured total in a simple bucket (evaporation is prevented with an appropriate substance such as mineral oil)? Drip from overhanging foliage and trees can augment precipitation totals.

D.3.2.3. Precipitation (frozen): Calm locations or shielding are a must. Undercatch for rain is only about 5 percent, but with winds of only 2–4 m/s, gauges may catch only 30–70 percent of the actual snow falling depending on density of the flakes. To catch 100 percent of the snow, the standard configuration for shielding is employed by the CRN (Climate Reference Network): the DFIR (Double-Fence Intercomparison Reference) shield with 2.4-m (8-ft.) vertical, wooden slatted fences in two concentric octagons with diameters of 8 m and 4 m (26 ft and 13 ft, respectively) and an inner Alter shield (flapping vanes). Numerous tests have shown this is the only way to achieve complete catch of snowfall (e.g., Yang et al. 1998, 2001). The DFIR shield is large and bulky; it is recommended that all precipitation gauges have at least Alter shields on them.

Near oceans, much snow is heavy and falls more vertically. In colder locations or storms, light flakes frequently will fly in and then out of the gauge. Clearings in forests are usually excellent sites. Snow blowing from trees that are too close can augment actual precipitation totals. Artificial shielding (vanes, etc.) placed around gauges in snowy locales always should be used if accurate totals are desired. Moving parts tend to freeze up. Capping of gauges during heavy snowfall events is a common occurrence. When the cap becomes pointed, snow falls off to the ground and is not recorded. Caps and plugs often will not fall into the tube until hours, days, or even weeks have passed, typically during an extended period of freezing temperature or above or when sunlight finally occurs. Liquid-based measurements (e.g., SNOTEL "rocket" gauges) do not have the resolution (usually 0.3 cm [0.1 in.] rather than 0.03 cm [0.01 in.]) that tipping bucket and other gauges have but are known to be reasonably accurate in very snowy climates. Light snowfall events might not be recorded until enough of them add up to the next reporting increment. More expensive gauges like Geonors can be considered and could do quite well in snowy settings; however, they need to be emptied every 40 cm (15 in.) or so (capacity of 51 cm [20 in.]) until the new 91-cm (36-in.) capacity gauge is offered for sale. Recently, the NWS has been trying out the new (and very expensive) Ott all-weather gauge. Riming can be an issue in windy foggy environments below freezing. Rime, dew, and other forms of atmospheric condensation are not real precipitation, since they are caused by the gauge.

D.3.2.4. Snow Depth: Windswept areas tend to be blown clear of snow. Conversely, certain types of vegetation can act as a snow fence and cause artificial drifts. However, some amount of vegetation in the vicinity generally can help slow down the wind. The two most common types of snow-depth gauges are the Judd Snow Depth Sensor, produced by Judd Communications, and the snow depth gauge produced by Campbell Scientific, Inc. Opinions vary on which one is better. These gauges use ultrasound and look downward in a cone about 22 degrees in diameter. The ground should be relatively clear of vegetation and maintained in a manner so that the zero point on the calibration scale does not change.

D.3.2.5. Snow Water Equivalent: This is determined by the weight of snow on fluid-filled pads about the size of a desktop set up sometimes in groups of four or in larger hexagons several meters in diameter. These pads require flat ground some distance from nearby sources of windblown snow and shielding that is "just right": not too close to the shielding to act as a kind of snow fence and not too far from the shielding so that blowing and drifting become a factor. Generally, these pads require fluids that possess antifreeze-like properties, as well as handling and replacement protocols.

D.3.2.6. Wind: Open exposures are needed for wind measurements. Small prominences or benches without blockage from certain sectors are preferred. A typical rule for trees is to site stations back 10 tree-heights from all tree obstructions. Sites in long, narrow valleys can obviously only exhibit two main wind directions. Gently rounded eminences are more favored. Any kind of topographic steering should be avoided to the extent possible. Avoiding major mountain chains or single isolated mountains or ridges is usually a favorable approach, if there is a choice. Sustained wind speed and the highest gusts (1-second) should be recorded. Averaging methodologies for both sustained winds and gusts can affect climate trends and should be recorded as metadata with all changes noted. Vegetation growth affects the vertical wind profile, and growth over a few years can lead to changes in mean wind speed even if the "real" wind does not change, so vegetation near the site (perhaps out to 50 m) should be maintained in a quasi-permanent status (same height and spatial distribution). Wind devices can rime up and freeze or spin out of balance. In severely rimed or windy climates, rugged anemometers, such as those made by Taylor, are worth considering. These anemometers are expensive but durable and can withstand substantial abuse. In exposed locations, personnel should plan for winds to be at least 50 m/s and be able to measure these wind speeds. At a minimum, anemometers should be rated to 75 m/s.

D.3.2.7. Humidity: Humidity is a relatively straightforward climate element. Close proximity to lakes or other water features can affect readings. Humidity readings typically are less accurate near 100 percent and at low humidities in cold weather.

D.3.2.8. Solar Radiation: A site with an unobstructed horizon obviously is the most desirable. This generally implies a flat plateau or summit. However, in most locations trees or mountains will obstruct the sun for part of the day.

D.3.2.9. Soil Temperature: It is desirable to measure soil temperature at locations where soil is present. If soil temperature is recorded at only a single depth, the most preferred depth is 10 cm. Other common depths include 25 cm, 50 cm, 2 cm, and 100 cm. Biological activity in the soil will be proportional to temperature with important threshold effects occurring near freezing.

D.3.2.10. Soil Moisture: Soil-moisture gauges are somewhat temperamental and require care to install. The soil should be characterized by a soil expert during installation of the gauge. The readings may require a certain level of experience to interpret correctly. If accurate, readings of soil moisture are especially useful.

D.3.2.11. Distributed Observations: It can be seen readily that compromises must be struck among the considerations described in the preceding paragraphs because some are mutually exclusive.

How large can a "site" be? Generally, the equipment footprint should be kept as small as practical with all components placed next to each other (within less than 10–20 m or so). Readings from one instrument frequently are used to aid in interpreting readings from the remaining instruments.

What is a tolerable degree of separation? Some consideration may be given to locating a precipitation gauge or snow pillow among protective vegetation, while the associated temperature, wind, and humidity readings would be collected more effectively in an open and exposed location within 20–50 m. Ideally, it is advantageous to know the wind measurement precisely at the precipitation gauge, but a compromise involving a short split, and in effect a "distributed observation," could be considered. There are no definitive rules governing this decision, but it is suggested that the site footprint be kept within approximately 50 m. There also are constraints imposed by engineering and electrical factors that affect cable lengths, signal strength, and line noise; therefore, the shorter the cable the better. Practical issues include the need to trench a channel to outlying instruments or to allow lines to lie atop the ground and associated problems with animals, humans, weathering, etc. Separating a precipitation gauge up to 100 m or so from an instrument mast may be an acceptable compromise if other factors are not limiting.

D.3.2.12. Instrument Replacement Schedules:  Instruments slowly degrade, and a plan for replacing them with new, refurbished, or recalibrated instruments should be in place. After approximately five years, a systematic change-out procedure should result in replacing most sensors in a network. Certain parts, such as solar radiation sensors, are candidates for annual calibration or change-out. Anemometers tend to degrade as bearings erode or electrical contacts become uneven. Noisy bearings are an indication, and a stethoscope might aid in hearing such noises. Increased internal friction affects the threshold starting speed; once spinning, they tend to function properly. Increases in starting threshold speeds can lead to more zero-wind measurements and thus reduce the reported mean wind speed with no real change in wind properties. A field calibration kit should be developed and taken on all site visits, routine or otherwise. Rain gauges can be tested with drip testers during field visits. Protective conduit and tight water seals can prevent abrasion and moisture problems with the equipment, although seals can keep moisture in as well as out. Bulletproof casings sometimes are employed in remote settings. A supply of spare parts, at least one of each and more for less-expensive or more-delicate sensors, should be maintained to allow replacement of worn or nonfunctional instruments during field visits. In addition, this approach allows instruments to be calibrated in the relative convenience of the operational home—the larger the network, the greater the need for a parts depot.

### D.3.3. Long-Term Comparability and Consistency

D.3.3.1. Consistency:  The emphasis here is to hold biases constant. Every site has biases, problems, and idiosyncrasies of one sort or another. The best rule to follow is simply to try to keep biases constant through time. Since the goal is to track climate through time, keeping sensors, methodologies, and exposure constant will ensure that only true climate change is being measured. This means leaving the site in its original state or performing maintenance to keep it that way. Once a site is installed, the goal should be to never move the site even by a few meters or to allow significant changes to occur within 100 m for the next several decades.

Sites in or near rock outcroppings likely will experience less vegetative disturbance or growth through the years and will not usually retain moisture, a factor that could speed corrosion. Sites that will remain locally similar for some time are usually preferable. However, in some cases the intent of a station might be to record the local climate effects of changes within a small-scale system (for example, glacier, recently burned area, or scene of some other disturbance) that is subject to a regional climate influence. In this example, the local changes might be much larger than the regional changes.

D.3.3.2. Metadata:  Since the climate of every site is affected by features in the immediate vicinity, it is vital to record this information over time and to update the record repeatedly at each service visit. Distances, angles, heights of vegetation, fine-scale topography, condition of instruments, shielding discoloration, and other factors from within a meter to several kilometers should be noted. Systematic photography should be undertaken and updated at least once every one–two years.

Photographic documentation should be taken at each site in a standard manner and repeated every two–three years. Guidelines for methodology were developed by Redmond (2004) as a result of experience with the NOAA CRN and can be found on the WRCC NPS Web pages at http://www.wrcc.dri.edu/nps and at ftp://ftp.wrcc.dri.edu/nps/photodocumentation.pdf.

The main purpose for climate stations is to *track climatic conditions through time*. Anything that affects the interpretation of records through time must to be noted and recorded for posterity. The important factors should be clear to a person who has never visited the site, no matter how long ago the site was installed.

In regions with significant, climatic transition zones, transects are an efficient way to span several climates and make use of available resources. Discussions on this topic at greater detail can be found in Redmond and Simeral (2004) and in Redmond et al. (2005).

## D.4. Literature Cited

American Association of State Climatologists. 1985. Heights and exposure standards for sensors on automated weather stations. The State Climatologist **9**.

Brock, F. V., K. C. Crawford, R. L. Elliott, G. W. Cuperus, S. J. Stadler, H. L. Johnson and M. D. Eilts. 1995. The Oklahoma Mesonet: A technical overview. Journal of Atmospheric and Oceanic Technology **12**:5-19.

Daly, C., R. P. Neilson, and D. L. Phillips. 1994. A statistical-topographic model for mapping climatological precipitation over mountainous terrain. Journal of Applied Meteorology **33**:140-158.

Daly, C., W. P. Gibson, G. H. Taylor, G. L. Johnson, and P. Pasteris. 2002. A knowledge-based approach to the statistical mapping of climate. Climate Research **22**:99-113.

Doggett, M., C. Daly, J. Smith, W. Gibson, G. Taylor, G. Johnson, and P. Pasteris. 2004. High-resolution 1971-2000 mean monthly temperature maps for the western United States. Fourteenth AMS Conf. on Applied Climatology, 84th AMS Annual Meeting. Seattle, WA, American Meteorological Society, Boston, MA, January 2004, Paper 4.3, CD-ROM.

Geiger, R., R. H. Aron, and P. E. Todhunter. 2003. The Climate Near the Ground. 6th edition. Rowman & Littlefield Publishers, Inc., New York.

Gibson, W. P., C. Daly, T. Kittel, D. Nychka, C. Johns, N. Rosenbloom, A. McNab, and G. Taylor. 2002. Development of a 103-year high-resolution climate data set for the conterminous United States. Thirteenth AMS Conf. on Applied Climatology. Portland, OR, American Meteorological Society, Boston, MA, May 2002:181-183.

Goodison, B. E., P. Y. T. Louie, and D. Yang. 1998. WMO solid precipitation measurement intercomparison final report. WMO TD 982, World Meteorological Organization, Geneva, Switzerland.

National Research Council. 1998. Future of the National Weather Service Cooperative Weather Network. National Academies Press, Washington, D.C.

National Research Council. 2001. A Climate Services Vision: First Steps Toward the Future. National Academies Press, Washington, D.C.

Redmond, K. T. 1992. Effects of observation time on interpretation of climatic time series - A need for consistency. Eighth Annual Pacific Climate (PACLIM) Workshop. Pacific Grove, CA, March 1991:141-150.

Redmond, K. T. 2004. Photographic documentation of long-term climate stations. Available from ftp://ftp.wrcc.dri.edu/nps/photodocumentation.pdf. (accessed 15 August 2004)

Redmond, K. T. and D. B. Simeral. 2004. Climate monitoring comments: Central Alaska Network Inventory and Monitoring Program. Available from ftp://ftp.wrcc.dri.edu/nps/alaska/cakn/npscakncomments040406.pdf. (accessed 6 April 2004)

Redmond, K. T., D. B. Simeral, and G. D. McCurdy. 2005. Climate monitoring for southwest Alaska national parks: network design and site selection. Report 05-01. Western Regional Climate Center, Reno, Nevada.

Redmond, K. T., and G. D. McCurdy. 2005. Channel Islands National Park: Design considerations for weather and climate monitoring. Report 05-02. Western Regional Climate Center, Reno, Nevada.

Sevruk, B., and W. R. Hamon. 1984. International comparison of national precipitation gauges with a reference pit gauge. Instruments and Observing Methods, Report No 17, WMO/TD – 38, World Meteorological Organization, Geneva, Switzerland.

Simpson, J. J., Hufford, G. L., C. Daly, J. S. Berg, and M. D. Fleming. 2005. Comparing maps of mean monthly surface temperature and precipitation for Alaska and adjacent areas of Canada produced by two different methods. Arctic **58**:137-161.

Whiteman, C. D. 2000. Mountain Meteorology: Fundamentals and Applications. Oxford University Press, Oxford, UK.

Wilson, E. O. 1998. Consilience: The Unity of Knowledge. Knopf, New York.

World Meteorological Organization. 1983. Guide to meteorological instruments and methods of observation, No. 8, 5th edition, World Meteorological Organization, Geneva Switzerland.

World Meteorological Organization. 2005. Organization and planning of intercomparisons of rainfall intensity gauges. World Meteorological Organization, Geneva Switzerland.

Yang, D., B. E. Goodison, J. R. Metcalfe, V. S. Golubev, R. Bates, T. Pangburn, and C. Hanson. 1998. Accuracy of NWS 8" standard nonrecording precipitation gauge: results and application of WMO intercomparison. Journal of Atmospheric and Oceanic Technology **15**:54-68.

Yang, D., B. E. Goodison, J. R. Metcalfe, P. Louie, E. Elomaa, C. Hanson, V. Bolubev, T. Gunther, J. Milkovic, and M. Lapin. 2001. Compatibility evaluation of national precipitation gauge measurements. Journal of Geophysical Research **106**:1481-1491.

# Appendix E. Master metadata field list

| Field Name | Field Type | Field Description |
|---|---|---|
| begin_date | date | Effective beginning date for a record. |
| begin_date_flag | char(2) | Flag describing the known accuracy of the begin date for a station. |
| best_elevation | float(4) | Best known elevation for a station (in feet). |
| clim_div_code | char(2) | Foreign key defining climate division code (primary in table: clim_div). |
| clim_div_key | int2 | Foreign key defining climate division for a station (primary in table: clim_div. |
| clim_div_name | varchar(30) | English name for a climate division. |
| controller_info | varchar(50) | Person or organization who maintains the identifier system for a given weather or climate network. |
| country_key | int2 | Foreign key defining country where a station resides (primary in table: none). |
| county_key | int2 | Foreign key defining county where a station resides (primary in table: county). |
| county_name | varchar(31) | English name for a county. |
| description | text | Any description pertaining to the particular table. |
| end_date | date | Last effective date for a record. |
| end_date_flag | char(2) | Flag describing the known accuracy of station end date. |
| fips_country_code | char(2) | FIPS (federal information processing standards) country code. |
| fips_state_abbr | char(2) | FIPS state abbreviation for a station. |
| fips_state_code | char(2) | FIPS state code for a station. |
| history_flag | char(2) | Describes temporal significance of an individual record among others from the same station. |
| id_type_key | int2 | Foreign key defining the id_type for a station (usually defined in code). |
| last_updated | date | Date of last update for a record. |
| latitude | float(8) | Latitude value. |
| longitude | float(8) | Longitude value. |
| name_type_key | int2 | "3": COOP station name, "2": best station name. |
| name | varchar(30) | Station name as known at date of last update entry. |
| ncdc_state_code | char(2) | NCDC, two-character code identifying U.S. state. |
| network_code | char(8) | Eight-character abbreviation code identifying a network. |
| network_key | int2 | Foreign key defining the network for a station (primary in table: network). |
| network_station_id | int4 | Identifier for a station in the associated network, which is defined by id_type_key. |
| remark | varchar(254) | Additional information for a record. |
| src_quality_code | char(2) | Code describing the data quality for the data source. |
| state_key | int2 | Foreign key defining the U.S. state where a station resides (primary in table: state). |
| state_name | varchar(30) | English name for a state. |
| station_alt_name | varchar(30) | Other English names for a station. |
| station_best_name | varchar(30) | Best, most well-known English name for a station. |
| time_zone | float4 | Time zone where a station resides. |
| ucan_station_id | int4 | Unique station identifier for every station in ACIS. |
| unit_key | int2 | Integer value representing a unit of measure. |

| Field Name | Field Type | Field Description |
|---|---|---|
| updated_by | char(8) | Person who last updated a record. |
| var_major_id | int2 | Defines major climate variable. |
| var_minor_id | int2 | Defines data source within a var_major_id. |
| zipcode | char(5) | Zipcode where a latitude/longitude point resides. |
| nps_netcode | char(4) | Network four-character identifier. |
| nps_netname | varchar(128) | Displayed English name for a network. |
| parkcode | char(4) | Park four-character identifier. |
| parkname | varchar(128) | Displayed English name for a park/ |
| im_network | char(4) | NPS I&M network where park belongs (a net code)/ |
| station_id | varchar(16) | Station identifier. |
| station_id_type | varchar(16) | Type of station identifier. |
| network.subnetwork.id | varchar(16) | Identifier of a sub-network in associated network. |
| subnetwork_key | int2 | Foreign key defining sub-network for a station. |
| subnetwork_name | varchar(30) | English name for a sub-network. |
| slope | integer | Terrain slope at the location. |
| aspect | integer | Terrain aspect at the station. |
| gps | char(1) | Indicator of latitude/longitude recorded via GPS (global positioning system). |
| site_description | text(0) | Physical description of site. |
| route_directions | text(0) | Driving route or site access directions. |
| station_photo_id | integer | Unique identifier associating a group of photos to a station. Group of photos all taken on same date. |
| photo_id | char(30) | Unique identifier for a photo. |
| photo_date | datetime | Date photograph taken. |
| photographer | varchar(64) | Name of photographer. |
| maintenance_date | datetime | Date of station maintenance visit. |
| contact_key | Integer | Unique identifier associating contact information to a station. |
| full_name | varchar(64) | Full name of contact person. |
| organization | varchar(64) | Organization of contact person. |
| contact_type | varchar(32) | Type of contact person (operator, administrator, etc.) |
| position_title | varchar(32) | Title of contact person. |
| address | varchar(32) | Address for contact person. |
| city | varchar(32) | City for contact person. |
| state | varchar(2) | State for contact person. |
| zip_code | char(10) | Zipcode for contact person. |
| country | varchar(32) | Country for contact person. |
| email | varchar(64) | E-mail for contact person. |
| work_phone | varchar(16) | Work phone for contact person. |
| contact_notes | text(254) | Other details regarding contact person. |
| equipment_type | char(30) | Sensor measurement type; i.e., wind speed, air temperature, etc. |
| eq_manufacturer | char(30) | Manufacturer of equipment. |
| eq_model | char(20) | Model number of equipment. |
| serial_num | char(20) | Serial number of equipment. |
| eq_description | varchar(254) | Description of equipment. |
| install_date | datetime | Installation date of equipment. |
| remove_date | datetime | Removal date of equipment. |
| ref_height | integer | Sensor displacement height from surface. |
| sampling_interval | varchar(10) | Frequency of sensor measurement. |

# Appendix F. Electronic supplements

**F.1. ACIS metadata file** for weather and climate stations associated with the ROMN: http://www.wrcc.dri.edu/nps/pub/ROMN/metadata/ROMN_from_ACIS.tar.gz.

# Appendix G. Descriptions of weather/climate monitoring networks

## G.1. Pacific Northwest Cooperative Agricultural Network (AgriMet)

- Purpose of network: provide weather/climate data for regional crop water use modeling, frost monitoring, and various agricultural research projects in the Pacific Northwest.
- Primary management agency: BLM.
- Data website: http://www.usbr.gov/pn/agrimet/wxdata.html.
- Measured weather/climate elements:
  o Air temperature.
  o Relative humidity and dewpoint temperature.
  o Precipitation.
  o Wind speed.
  o Solar radiation.
- Sampling frequency: hourly.
- Reporting frequency: hourly; some stations report every 10 minutes if real-time communications are available.
- Estimated station cost: $12000 with maintenance costs around $2000/year.
- Network strengths:
  o AgriMet has near-real-time data.
  o Period of record is relatively long.
  o Sites are well maintained.
- Network weaknesses:
  o Only agricultural sites are sampled.
  o AgriMet has a limited geographic extent (Pacific Northwest).

AgriMet is a satellite-based network of automated weather stations operated by the BLM. Stations in AgriMet are located primarily in irrigated agricultural areas throughout the Pacific Northwest.

## G.2. NWS Forecast Office, Boulder, Colorado (BWFO)

- Purpose of network: provide near-real-time local meteorological data to assist in routine weather forecast development for northern Colorado.
- Primary management agency: NWS forecast office, Boulder, Colorado.
- Data website: http://www.met.utah.edu/jhorel/html/mesonet.
- Measured weather/climate elements:
  o Air temperature.
  o Relative humidity.
  o Precipitation.
  o Wind speed and direction.
  o Wind gust and direction.
- Sampling frequency: unknown.
- Reporting frequency: unknown.
- Estimated station cost: unknown.

- Network strengths:
  - Real-time data.
- Network weaknesses:
  - Uncertain data quality and station maintenance.
  - Coverage generally limited to northern Colorado.

These are near-real-time stations managed by the NWS forecast office in Boulder, Colorado. Data from these stations are used to provide local weather data to assist in developing routine weather forecasts for northern Colorado. Measured meteorological elements include temperature, precipitation, wind, and relative humidity.

## G.3. Canadian weather/climate stations (CANADA)

- Purpose of network: provide weather/climate data for forecasting and climate-monitoring efforts in Canada.
- Primary management agency: The Meteorological Service of Canada.
- Data website: http://www.weatheroffice.ec.gc.ca/canada_e.html.
- Measured weather/climate elements:
  - Air temperature.
  - Barometric pressure.
  - Relative humidity and dewpoint temperature.
  - Precipitation.
  - Wind speed and direction.
  - Wind gust and direction.
  - Solar radiation.
  - Sky Cover.
  - Ceiling.
  - Visibility.
- Sampling frequency: hourly.
- Reporting frequency: hourly.
- Estimated station cost: unknown.
- Network strengths:
  - Data are of high quality.
  - Periods of record are relatively long.
  - Sites are well maintained.
- Network weaknesses:
  - Sites are only in Canada, so usefulness limited to northern NPS park units.
  - Limited data access.

These include various automated weather/climate station networks from Canada. The Meteorological Service of Canada operates many of these stations, including airport sites. The data measured at these sites generally include temperature, precipitation, humidity, wind, barometric pressure, sky cover, ceiling, visibility, and current weather. Most of the data records are of high quality.

## G.4. Clean Air Status and Trends Network (CASTNet)

- Purpose of network: provide information for evaluating the effectiveness of national emission-control strategies.
- Primary management agency: EPA.
- Data website: http://epa.gov/castnet/.
- Measured weather/climate elements:
  - Air temperature.
  - Precipitation.
  - Relative humidity.
  - Wind speed.
  - Wind direction.
  - Wind gust.
  - Gust direction.
  - Solar radiation.
  - Soil moisture and temperature.
- Sampling frequency: hourly.
- Reporting frequency: hourly.
- Estimated station cost: $13000.
- Network strengths:
  - High-quality data.
  - Sites are well maintained.
- Network weaknesses:
  - Density of station coverage is low.
  - Shorter periods of record for western U.S.

The CASTNet network is primarily is an air-quality-monitoring network managed by the EPA. The elements shown here are intended to support interpretation of measured air-quality parameters such as ozone, nitrates, sulfides, etc., which also are measured at CASTNet sites.

## G.5. Colorado Department of Transportation (CDOT) Network

- Purpose of network: provide weather data to support management of Colorado's transportation network.
- Primary management agency: CDOT.
- Data website: http://www.met.utah.edu/jhorel/html/mesonet.
- Measured weather/climate elements:
  - Air temperature.
  - Relative humidity.
  - Barometric pressure.
  - Wind speed and direction.
  - Wind gust and direction.
- Sampling frequency: unknown.
- Reporting frequency: unknown.
- Estimated station cost: unknown.
- Network strengths:
  - Real-time data.

- Network weaknesses:
  o Coverage is limited to the state of Colorado.

These weather stations are operated by CDOT in support of management activities for Colorado's transportation network. Measured meteorological elements generally include temperature, precipitation, wind, and relative humidity.

## G.6. Colorado Agricultural Meteorological Network (CoAgMet)

- Purpose of network: provide weather data to support management of Colorado's transportation network.
- Primary management agencies: Colorado State University Extension Service; Colorado Climate Center.
- Data website: http://ccc.atmos.colostate.edu/~coagmet.
- Measured weather/climate elements:
  o Air temperature.
  o Relative humidity.
  o Precipitation.
  o Wind.
  o Solar radiation.
  o Soil temperature.
- Sampling frequency: unknown.
- Reporting frequency: hourly or daily.
- Estimated station cost: unknown.
- Network strengths:
  o Real-time data.
- Network weaknesses:
  o Coverage is limited to the state of Colorado.

The CoAgMet network is a weather monitoring network originally started in the early 1990s by the Agricultural Research Service branch of the USDA and the Plant Pathology extension service at Colorado State University. Data are managed by the Colorado Climate Center.

## G.7. NWS Cooperative Observer Program (COOP)

- Purpose of network:
  o Provide observational, meteorological data required to define U.S. climate and help measure long-term climate changes.
  o Provide observational, meteorological data in near real-time to support forecasting and warning mechanisms and other public service programs of the NWS.
- Primary management agency: NOAA (NWS).
- Data website: data are available from the NCDC (http://www.ncdc.noaa.gov), RCCs (e.g., WRCC, http://www.wrcc.dri.edu), and state climate offices.
- Measured weather/climate elements:
  o Maximum, minimum, and observation-time temperature.
  o Precipitation, snowfall, snow depth.
  o Pan evaporation (some stations).

- Sampling frequency: daily.
- Reporting frequency: daily or monthly (station-dependent).
- Estimated station cost: $2000 with maintenance costs of $500–900/year.
- Network strengths:
  - Decade–century records at most sites.
  - Widespread national coverage (thousands of stations).
  - Excellent data quality when well maintained.
  - Relatively inexpensive; highly cost effective.
  - Manual measurements; not automated.
- Network weaknesses:
  - Uneven exposures; many are not well-maintained.
  - Dependence on schedules for volunteer observers.
  - Slow entry of data from many stations into national archives.
  - Data subject to observational methodology; not always documented.
  - Manual measurements; not automated and not hourly.

The COOP network has long served as the main climate observation network in the U.S. Readings are usually made by volunteers using equipment supplied, installed, and maintained by the federal government. The observer in effect acts as a host for the data-gathering activities and supplies the labor; this is truly a "cooperative" effort. The SAO sites often are considered to be part of the cooperative network as well if they collect the previously mentioned types of weather/climate observations. Typical observation days are morning to morning, evening to evening, or midnight to midnight. By convention, observations are ascribed to the date the instrument was reset at the end of the observational period. For this reason, midnight observations represent the end of a day. The Historical Climate Network is a subset of the cooperative network but contains longer and more complete records.

## G.8. Colorado River Basin Forecast Center (CRBFC) Network

- Purpose of network: provide weather data for river forecasting efforts in Colorado River Basin.
- Data website: http://www.met.utah.edu/jhorel/html/mesonet.
- Measured weather/climate elements:
  - Air temperature.
  - Precipitation.
- Sampling frequency: hourly.
- Reporting frequency: hourly.
- Estimated station cost: unknown.
- Network strengths:
  - Data are in near-real-time.
- Network weaknesses:
  - Instrumentation platforms do sometimes vary.

The CRBFC network has over 100 weather stations in the Colorado River Basin. The primary purpose of CRBFC stations is to collect meteorological data in support of efforts by the CRBFC to monitor potential flood conditions in the Colorado River Basin.

## G.9. Citizen Weather Observer Program (CWOP)

- Purpose of network: collect observations from private citizens and make these data available for homeland security and other weather applications, providing constant feedback to the observers to maintain high data quality.
- Primary management agency: NOAA MADIS program.
- Data Website: http://www.wxqa.com.
- Measured weather/climate elements:
  o Air temperature.
  o Dewpoint temperature.
  o Precipitation.
  o Wind speed and direction.
  o Barometric pressure.
- Sampling frequency: 15 minutes or less.
- Reporting frequency: 15 minutes.
- Estimated station cost: unknown.
- Network strengths:
  o Active partnership between public agencies and private citizens.
  o Large number of participant sites.
  o Regular communications between data providers and users, encouraging higher data quality.
- Network weaknesses:
  o Variable instrumentation platforms.
  o Metadata are sometimes limited.

The CWOP network is a public-private partnership with U.S. citizens and various agencies including NOAA, NASA (National Aeronautics and Space Administration), and various universities. There are over 4500 registered sites worldwide, with close to 3000 of these sites located in North America.

## G.10. Denver Urban Drainage and Flood Control District (DUDFCD) Network

- Purpose of network: provide weather data for flash flood monitoring activities in the metropolitan area of Denver, Colorado.
- Primary management agency: City and County of Denver.
- Data website: http://www.met.utah.edu/jhorel/html/mesonet.
- Measured weather/climate elements:
  o Precipitation.
- Sampling frequency: unknown.
- Reporting frequency: once or twice daily.
- Estimated station cost: unknown.
- Network strengths:
  o Network coverage is dense.
- Network weaknesses:
  o Limited spatial extent.
  o Limited meteorological elements measured.

The DUDFCD operates a set of weather stations whose primary purpose is to collect near-real-time precipitation measurements in support of efforts by the DUDFCD to manage and monitor potential flood conditions in the Denver metropolitan area.

## G.11. Glacier National Park network (GNP)

- Purpose of network: provide weather data for GLAC.
- Data website: http://www.met.utah.edu/jhorel/html/mesonet.
- Measured weather/climate elements:
  o Air temperature.
  o Relative humidity.
  o Precipitation.
  o Wind.
  o Barometric pressure.
- Sampling frequency: hourly.
- Reporting frequency: hourly.
- Estimated station cost: unknown.
- Network strengths:
  o Data are in near-real-time.
  o Provides coverage at key locations in GLAC.
- Network weaknesses:
  o Spatial coverage is still quite limited.

The GNP network is a local network of weather/climate stations operated by GLAC. The primary purpose of these stations is to provide local meteorological data for GLAC.

## G.12. NPS Gaseous Pollutant Monitoring Program (GPMP)

- Purpose of network: measurement of ozone and related meteorological elements.
- Primary management agency: NPS.
- Data website: http://www2.nature.nps.gov/air/monitoring.
- Measured weather/climate elements:
  o Air temperature.
  o Relative humidity.
  o Precipitation.
  o Wind speed and direction.
  o Solar radiation.
  o Surface wetness.
- Sampling frequency: continuous.
- Reporting frequency: hourly.
- Estimated station cost: unknown.
- Network strengths:
  o Stations are located within NPS park units.
  o Data quality is excellent, with high data standards.
  o Provides unique measurements that are not available elsewhere.
  o Records are up to 2 decades in length.

- o Site maintenance is excellent.
- o Thermometers are aspirated.
  - Network weaknesses:
    - o Not easy to download the entire data set or to ingest live data.
    - o Period of record is short compared to other automated networks.
    - o Station spacing and coverage: station installation is episodic, driven by opportunistic situations.

The NPS web site indicates that there are 33 sites with continuous ozone analysis run by NPS, with records from a few to about 16-17 years. Of these stations, 12 are labeled as GPMP sites and the rest are labeled as CASTNet sites. All of these have standard meteorological measurements, including a 10-m mast. Another nine GPMP sites are located within NPS units but run by cooperating agencies. A number of other sites (1-2 dozen) ran for differing periods in the past, generally less than 5-10 years.

## G.13. NOAA Ground-Based GPS Meteorology (GPS-MET) Network

- Purpose of network:
  - o Measure atmospheric water vapor using ground-based GPS receivers.
  - o Facilitate use of these data operational and in other research and applications.
  - o Provides data for weather forecasting, atmospheric modeling and prediction, climate monitoring, calibrating and validation other observing systems including radiosondes and satellites, and research.
- Primary management agency: NOAA Earth System Research Laboratory.
- Data website: http://gpsmet.noaa.gov/jsp/index.jsp.
- Measurements:
  - o Dual frequency carrier phase measurements every 30 seconds.
- Ancillary weather/climate observations:
  - o Air temperature.
  - o Relative humidity.
  - o Barometric pressure.
- Reporting frequency: currently 30 min.
- Estimated station cost: $0-$10000, depending on approach. Data from dual frequency GPS receivers installed for conventional applications (e.g., high accuracy surveying) can be used without modification.
- Network strengths:
  - o Frequent, high-quality measurements.
  - o High reliability.
  - o All-weather operability.
  - o Many uses.
  - o Highly leveraged.
  - o Requires no calibration.
  - o Measurement accuracy improves with time.
- Network weakness:
  - o Point measurement.
  - o Provides no direct information about the vertical distribution of water vapor.

The GPS-MET network is the first network of its kind dedicated to GPS meteorology (see Duan et al. 1996). The GPS-MET network was developed in response to the need for improved moisture observations to support weather forecasting, climate monitoring, and other research activities. GPS-MET is a collaboration between NOAA and several other governmental and university organizations and institutions.

GPS meteorology utilizes the radio signals broadcast by the satellite Global Positioning System for atmospheric remote sensing. GPS meteorology applications have evolved along two paths: ground-based (Bevis et al. 1992) and space-based (Yuan et al. 1993). Both applications make the same fundamental measurement (the apparent delay in the arrival of radio signals caused by changes in the radio-refractivity of the atmosphere along the paths of the radio signals) but they do so from different perspectives.

In ground-based GPS meteorology, a GPS receiver and antenna are placed at a fixed location on the ground and the signals from all GPS satellites in view are continuously recorded. From this information, the exact position of the GPS antenna can be determined over time with high (millimeter-level) accuracy. Subsequent measurements of the antenna position are compared with the known position, and the differences can be attributed to changes in the temperature, pressure and water vapor in the atmosphere above the antenna. By making continuous measurements of temperature and pressure at the site, the total amount of water vapor in the atmosphere at this location can be estimated with high accuracy under all weather conditions. For more information on ground based GPS meteorology the reader is referred to http://gpsmet.noaa.gov.

In space-based GPS meteorology, GPS receivers and antennas are placed on satellites in Low Earth Orbit (LEO), and the signals transmitted by a GPS satellite are continuously recorded as a GPS satellite "rises" or "sets" behind the limb of the Earth. This process is called an occultation or a limb sounding. The GPS radio signals bend more as they encounter a thicker atmosphere and the bending (which causes an apparent increase in the length of the path of the radio signal) can be attributed to changes in temperature, pressure and water vapor along the path of the radio signal through the atmosphere that is nominally about 300 km long. The location of an occultation depends on the relative geometries of the GPS satellites in Mid Earth Orbit and the satellites in LEO. As a consequence, information about the vertical temperature, pressure and moisture structure of the Earth's atmosphere as a whole can be estimated with high accuracy, but not at any one particular place over time. The main difference between ground and space-based GPS meteorology is one of geometry. A space-based measurement can be thought of as a ground-based measurement turned on its side. For more information on space based GPS meteorology, the reader is referred to http://www.cosmic.ucar.edu/gpsmet/.

## G.14. U.S. Long Term Ecological Research (LTER) Network

- Purpose of network: provide weather and climate data for ecological research activities at LTER sites around the U.S.
- Data website: http://www.lternet.edu.
- Measured weather/climate elements:
  o Air temperature.

o Relative humidity and dewpoint temperature.
o Precipitation.
o Wind.
- Sampling frequency: unknown.
- Reporting frequency: hourly.
- Estimated station cost: unknown.
- Network strengths:
  o Data are in near-real-time.
  o Data are usually of very high quality.
- Network weaknesses:
  o Limited national coverage (only at designated LTER sites, e.g., Niwot Ridge).

The LTER network started in 1980 and is a collaborative effort among ecologists around the U.S. to investigate ecological processes over a wide range of spatial and temporal scales. Near-real-time climate elements are measured at LTER sites in support of ongoing ecological research efforts.

## G.15. NWS Forecast Office, Missoula, Montana (MSOWFO)

- Purpose of network: provide near-real-time local meteorological data to assist in routine weather forecast development for western Montana.
- Primary management agency: NWS forecast office, Missoula, Montana.
- Data website: http://www.met.utah.edu/jhorel/html/mesonet.
- Measured weather/climate elements:
  o Air temperature.
  o Relative humidity.
  o Precipitation.
  o Wind speed and direction.
  o Wind gust and direction.
- Sampling frequency: unknown.
- Reporting frequency: unknown.
- Estimated station cost: unknown.
- Network strengths:
  o Real-time data.
- Network weaknesses:
  o Uncertain data quality and station maintenance.
  o Coverage limited to western Montana.

These are near-real-time stations managed by the NWS forecast office in Missoula, Montana. Data from these stations are used to provide local weather data to assist in developing routine weather forecasts for western Montana. Measured meteorological elements include temperature, precipitation, wind, and relative humidity.

## G.16. Montana Department of Transportation (MT DOT) Network

- Purpose of network: provide weather data to support management of Montana's transportation network.

103

- Primary management agency: MT DOT.
- Data website: http://www.met.utah.edu/jhorel/html/mesonet.
- Measured weather/climate elements:
  o Air temperature.
  o Relative humidity.
  o Barometric pressure.
  o Wind speed and direction.
  o Wind gust and direction.
- Sampling frequency: unknown.
- Reporting frequency: unknown.
- Estimated station cost: unknown.
- Network strengths:
  o Real-time data.
- Network weaknesses:
  o Coverage is limited to the state of Montana.

These weather stations are operated by MT DOT in support of management activities for Montana's transportation network. Measured meteorological elements generally include temperature, precipitation, wind, and relative humidity.

## G.17. National Atmospheric Deposition Program (NADP)

- Purpose of network: measurement of precipitation chemistry and atmospheric deposition.
- Primary management agencies: USDA, but multiple collaborators.
- Data website: http://nadp.sws.uiuc.edu.
- Measured weather/climate elements:
  o Precipitation.
- Sampling frequency: daily.
- Reporting frequency: daily.
- Estimated station cost: unknown.
- Network strengths:
  o Data quality is excellent, with high data standards.
  o Site maintenance is excellent.
- Network weaknesses:
  o A very limited number of climate parameters are measured.

Stations within the NADP network monitor primarily wet deposition through precipitation chemistry at selected sites around the U.S. and its territories. The network is a collaborative effort among several agencies including USGS and USDA. Precipitation is the primary climate parameter measured at NADP sites. This network includes MDN stations.

## G.18. USDA/NRCS Snowcourse Network (NRCS-SC)

- Purpose of network: collect snowpack and related climate data to assist in forecasting water supply in the western U.S.

- Primary management agency: NRCS.
- Data website: http://www.wcc.nrcs.usda.gov/snowcourse/.
- Measured weather/climate elements:
  - Snow depth.
  - Snow water equivalent.
- Sampling, reporting frequency: monthly or seasonally.
- Estimated station cost: cost of man-hours needed to set up snowcourse and make measurements.
- Network strengths:
  - Periods of record are generally long.
  - Large number of high-altitude sites.
- Network weaknesses:
  - Measurement and reporting only occurs on monthly to seasonal basis.
  - Few weather/climate elements are measured.

USDA/NRCS maintains a network of snow-monitoring stations known as snowcourses. Many of these sites have been in operation since the early part of the twentieth century. These are all manual sites where only snow depth and snow water content are measured.

## G.19. Portable Ozone Monitoring System (POMS)

- Purpose of network: provide seasonal, short-term (1-5 years) monitoring of near-surface atmospheric ozone levels in remote locations.
- Primary management agency: NPS.
- Data website: http://www2.nature.nps.gov/air/studies/portO3.htm.
- Measured weather/climate elements:
  - Air temperature.
  - Precipitation.
  - Relative humidity.
  - Wind speed and direction.
  - Solar radiation.
- Sampling frequency: hourly.
- Reporting frequency: hourly.
- Estimated station cost: $20000 with operation and maintenance costs of up to $10000/year.
- Network strengths:
  - High-quality data.
  - Site maintenance is excellent.
- Network weaknesses:
  - No long-term sites, so not as useful for climate monitoring.
  - Sites are somewhat expensive to operate.

The POMS network is operated by the NPS Air Resources Division. Sites are intended primarily for summer, short-term (1-5 years) monitoring of near-surface atmospheric ozone levels in remote locations. Measured meteorological elements include temperature, precipitation, wind, relative humidity, and solar radiation.

## G.20. Remote Automated Weather Station (RAWS) Network

- Purpose of network: provide near-real-time (hourly or near hourly) measurements of meteorological variables for use in fire weather forecasts and climatology. Data from RAWS also are used for natural resource management, flood forecasting, natural hazard management, and air-quality monitoring.
- Primary management agency: WRCC, National Interagency Fire Center.
- Data website: http://www.raws.dri.edu/index.html.
- Measured weather/climate elements:
  - Air temperature.
  - Precipitation.
  - Relative humidity.
  - Wind speed.
  - Wind direction.
  - Wind gust.
  - Gust direction.
  - Solar radiation.
  - Soil moisture and temperature.
- Sampling frequency: 1 or 10 minutes, element-dependent.
- Reporting frequency: generally hourly. Some stations report every 15 or 30 minutes.
- Estimated station cost: $12000 with satellite telemetry ($8000 without satellite telemetry); maintenance costs are around $2000/year.
- Network strengths:
  - Metadata records are usually complete.
  - Sites are located in remote areas.
  - Sites are generally well-maintained.
  - Entire period of record available on-line.
- Network weaknesses:
  - RAWS network is focused largely on fire management needs (formerly focused only on fire needs).
  - Frozen precipitation is not measured reliably.
  - Station operation is not always continuous.
  - Data transmission is completed via one-way telemetry. Data are therefore recoverable either in real-time or not at all.

The RAWS network is used by many land-management agencies, such as the BLM, NPS, Fish and Wildlife Service, Bureau of Indian Affairs, Forest Service, and other agencies. The RAWS network was one of the first automated weather station networks to be installed in the U.S. Most gauges do not have heaters, so hydrologic measurements are of little value when temperatures dip below freezing or reach freezing after frozen precipitation events. There are approximately 1100 real-time sites in this network and about 1800 historic sites (some are decommissioned or moved). The sites can transmit data all winter but may be in deep snow in some locations. The WRCC is the archive for this network and receives station data and metadata through a special connection to the National Interagency Fire Center in Boise, Idaho.

## G.21. NWS/FAA Surface Airways Observation Network (SAO)

- Purpose of network: provide near-real-time (hourly or near hourly) measurements of meteorological variables and are used both for airport operations and weather forecasting.
- Primary management agency: NOAA, FAA.
- Data website: data are available from state climate offices, RCCs (e.g., WRCC, http://www.wrcc.dri.edu), and NCDC (http://www.ncdc.noaa.gov).
- Measured weather/climate elements:
  - Air temperature.
  - Dewpoint and/or relative humidity.
  - Wind speed.
  - Wind direction.
  - Wind gust.
  - Gust direction.
  - Barometric pressure.
  - Precipitation (not at many FAA sites).
  - Sky cover.
  - Ceiling (cloud height).
  - Visibility.
- Sampling frequency: element-dependent.
- Reporting frequency: element-dependent.
- Estimated station cost: $100000–$200000, with maintenance costs approximately $10000/year.
- Network strengths:
  - Records generally extend over several decades.
  - Consistent maintenance and station operations.
  - Data record is reasonably complete and usually high quality.
  - Hourly or sub-hourly data.
- Network weaknesses:
  - Nearly all sites are located at airports.
  - Data quality can be related to size of airport—smaller airports tend to have poorer datasets.
  - Influences from urbanization and other land-use changes.

These stations are managed by NOAA, U. S. Navy, U. S. Air Force, and FAA. These stations are located generally at major airports and military bases. The FAA stations often do not record precipitation, or they may provide precipitation records of reduced quality. Automated stations are typically ASOSs for the NWS or AWOSs for the FAA. Some sites only report episodically with observers paid per observation.

## G.22. USDA/NRCS Snowfall Telemetry (SNOTEL) network

- Purpose of network: collect snowpack and related climate data to assist in forecasting water supply in the western U.S.
- Primary management agency: NRCS.
- Data website: http://www.wcc.nrcs.usda.gov/snow/.
- Measured weather/climate elements:

o Air temperature.
o Precipitation.
o Snow water content.
o Snow depth.
o Relative humidity (enhanced sites only).
o Wind speed (enhanced sites only).
o Wind direction (enhanced sites only).
o Solar radiation (enhanced sites only).
o Soil moisture and temperature (enhanced sites only).

- Sampling frequency: 1-minute temperature; 1-hour precipitation, snow water content, and snow depth. Less than one minute for relative humidity, wind speed and direction, solar radiation, and soil moisture and temperature (all at enhanced site configurations only).
- Reporting frequency: reporting intervals are user-selectable. Commonly used intervals are every one, two, three, or six hours.
- Estimated station cost: $20000 with maintenance costs approximately $2000/year.
- Network strengths:
  o Sites are located in high-altitude areas that typically do not have other weather or climate stations.
  o Data are of high quality and are largely complete.
  o Very reliable automated system.
- Network weaknesses:
  o Historically limited number of elements.
  o Remote so data gaps can be long.
  o Metadata sparse and not high quality; site histories are lacking.
  o Measurement and reporting frequencies vary.
  o Many hundreds of mountain ranges still not sampled.
  o Earliest stations were installed in the late 1970s; temperatures have only been recorded since the 1980s.

USDA/NRCS maintains a set of automated snow-monitoring stations known as the SNOTEL (snowfall telemetry) network. These stations are designed specifically for cold and snowy locations. Precipitation and snow water content measurements are intended for hydrologic applications and water-supply forecasting, so these measurements are measured generally to within 2.5 mm (0.1 in.). Snow depth is tracked to the nearest 25 mm, or one inch. These stations function year around.

### G.23. Weather For You (WX4U) network

- Purpose of network: allow volunteer weather enthusiasts around the U.S. to observe and share weather data.
- Data website: http://www.met.utah.edu/jhorel/html/mesonet.
- Measured weather/climate elements:
  o Air temperature.
  o Relative humidity and dewpoint temperature.
  o Precipitation.
  o Wind speed and direction.
  o Wind gust and direction.

- o Barometric pressure.
- Sampling frequency: 10 minutes.
- Reporting frequency: 10 minutes.
- Estimated station cost: unknown.
- Network strengths:
  - o Stations are located throughout the U.S.
  - o Stations provide near-real-time observations.
- Network weaknesses:
  - o Instrumentation platforms can be variable.
  - o Data are sometimes of questionable quality.

The WX4U network is a nationwide collection of weather stations run by local observers. Meteorological elements that are measured usually include temperature, precipitation, wind, and humidity.

NPS/ROMN/NRTR—2007/036, May 2007